Expository Discourse

Open Linguistics Series

Series Editor
Robin Fawcett, Cardiff University

This series is 'open' in two related ways. First, it is not confined to works associated with any one school of linguistics. For almost two decades the series has played a significant role in establishing and maintaining the present climate of 'openness' in linguistics, and we intend to maintain this tradition. However, we particularly welcome works which explore the nature and use of language through modelling its potential for use in social contexts, or through a cognitive model of language – or indeed a combination of the two.

The series is also 'open' in the sense that it welcomes works that open out 'core' linguistics in various ways: to give the description of natural texts and the use of corpora a central place; to encompass discourse 'above the sentence'; to relate language to other semiotic systems; to apply linguistics in fields such as education, language pathology, and law; and to explore the areas that lie btween linguistics and its neighbouring disciplines such as psychology, sociology, philosophy, and cultural and literary studies.

Continuum also publishes a series that offers a forum for primarily functional descriptions of languages or parts of languages – *Functional Descriptions of Language*. Relations between linguistics and computing are covered in the *Communication in Artificial Intelligence* series, two series, *Advances in Applied Linguistics* and *Communication in Public Life*, publish books in applied linguistics and the series *Modern Pragmatics in Theory and Practice* publishes both social and cognitive perspectives on the making of meaning in language use. We also publish a range of introductory textbooks on topics in linguistics, semiotics and deaf studies.

Recent titles in this series

Construing Experience through Meaning: A Language-based Approach to Cognition,
    M. A. K. Halliday and Christian M. I. M. Matthiessen
Culturally Speaking: Managing Rapport through Talk across Cultures, Helen Spencer-Oatey (ed.)
Educating Eve: The 'Language Instinct' Debate, Geoffrey Sampson
Empirical Linguistics, Geoffrey Sampson
Genre and Institutions: Social Processes in the Workplace and School, Frances Christie and
    J. R. Martin (eds)
The Intonation Systems of English, Paul Tench
Language Policy in Britain and France: The Processes of Policy, Dennis Ager
Language Relations across Bering Strait: Reappraising the Archaeological and Linguistic Evidence,
    Michael Fortescue
Learning through Language in Early Childhood, Clare Painter
Pedagogy and the Shaping of Consciousness: Linguistic and Social Processes, Frances Christie (ed.)
Register Analysis: Theory and Practice, Mohsen Ghadessy (ed.)
Researching Language in Schools and Communities: Functional Linguistic Perspectives,
    Len Unsworth (ed.)
Summary Justice: Judges Address Juries, Paul Robertshaw
Thematic Developments in English Texts, Mohsen Ghadessy (ed.)
Ways of Saying: Ways of Meaning. Selected Papers of Ruqaiya Hasan, Carmen Cloran,
    David Butt and Geoffrey Williams (eds)
Words, Meaning and Vocabulary: An Introduction to Modern English Lexicology, Howard Jackson
    and Etienne Zé Amvela

Expository Discourse

A Genre-based Approach to Social Science Research Texts

Beverly A. Lewin, Jonathan Fine
and Lynne Young

CONTINUUM
London and New York

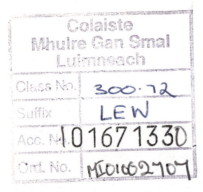
Continuum
The Tower Building, 11 York Road, London SE1 7NX
370 Lexington Aveue, New York, NY 10017-6503

First published 2001

British Library Cataloguing-in-Publication Data
A catalogue record for this book is available from the British Library.

ISBN 0-8264-4913-1 (hardback)

Library of Congress Cataloging-in-Publication Data
Lewin, Beverly A. 1937–
    Expository discourse: a genre-based approach to social science research texts / Beverly
A. Lewin, Jonathan Fine, Lynne Young.
        p. cm.
    Includes bibliographical references and index.
    ISBN 0-8264-4913-1 (hardcover)
        1. Social sciences—Research. I. Fine, Jonathan. II. Young, Lynne. III. Title

H62 .L446 2001
300'.7'2—dc21

                                                                        00-048391

Typeset by CentraServe, Saffron Walden, Essex
Printed and bound in Great Britain by TJ International, Padstow

Contents

List of tables

List of figures

Acknowledgements

This work, based on the PhD dissertation of Beverly Lewin, has been extensively rewritten and revised by all three authors.

Lynne Young would like to thank her husband, Bill Young, for his patience throughout this project and for his many helpful comments. Jonathan Fine would like to thank his family for their forbearance with the time and energy this effort absorbed, even during the most trying times for all. Beverly Lewin would like to thank Lawrence, Alisa, Ilana and Josh Lewin for constant encouragement and for putting up with her preoccupation with scientific writing.

We would all like to express our gratitude to Juliann Clatworthy-Smith, who prepared the manuscript for submission and cheerfully put up with many changes. A special thanks to Josh Lewin, who prepared the flowchart for us. Last but not least, we would all like to thank one another.

July 2000

1 A critical review of genre analysis

Preface

The purpose of our work is first to contribute to a comprehensive model of genre in expository texts, showing the interweaving of genre, registerial and discoursal options. Although different aspects of texts have been carefully described, these analyses, with significant exceptions, e.g. Ventola (1987), have stopped short of showing how systems interact within the same text.

Our second goal is to apply this model to the characterization of social science research texts in particular. Our intention, then, is to illustrate a particular approach to the study of genre through the detailed examination of social science research texts in particular. The purpose is not only to demonstrate the application of a model to a specific field of study but also to characterize an academic domain that has been neglected in genre studies, which have concentrated on physical sciences. Such an approach in our study has yielded, as we will outline in the coming chapters, a more complete characterization of the genre of social science research (SSR) texts than studies that focus only on one system or aspect. The information provided by the interaction of systems within texts, combined with the knowledge of context provided by registerial constructs, allowed us to fully characterize one generic variety and its generic structure. Such identification enables researchers to make predictions about constitutive elements of different genres.

The study of genre has become centred primarily in four areas of rather diverse research: systemic linguistics, genre studies, writing and ESP (English for Specific Purposes). Our work has been influenced by each of these to differing degrees. The systems of networks with which we describe our data are based on work by systemic linguists such as Halliday, Hasan, Martin and Ventola; of similar significance is the work of genre analysis by ESP specialists as represented primarily by Swales. The tradition of writing with which we have been concerned is the approach adopted by Bazerman in his study of the evolution of writing in scientific texts in which he examined the changing nature of scientific research articles as they evolved to answer changing social needs.

* * *

The current study, like others in genre analysis, has arisen from an understanding that communicative events are accomplished by a series of interlocking acts realized linguistically. Such information has led practitioners in the field of English for Specific Purposes and English for Academic Purposes to realize that it is not sufficient to teach their students to encode and decode individual units of meaning in sentences. They have become aware of the need to broaden their syllabi to include the conventional types and sequences of acts involved in participating in particular communicative events, e.g. book reviews and laboratory demonstrations (Fortanet *et al.*, 1998). This also facilitates student recognition of how texts accomplish personal and social purposes. This knowledge is particularly important given the increasing numbers of non-native speakers who are learning to read and, often, write scientific works in English. The analysis and identification of the units which comprise specific genres should further these educational purposes.

The teaching of English for Specific Purposes by two of the authors has also sensitized us to the needs of tertiary-level language learners as they learn to read and write within the scientific community. The aim of our model, then, is to demonstrate a systematic method for characterizing genre in expository texts which could serve as an archetype for more thorough descriptions of a variety of scientific genres. We are, however, as teachers and researchers, well aware that in the past theoretical and descriptive findings have often been directly applied to classroom use without uniform success. Because of this, we would suggest that while the present work may indicate many directions for teachers and curriculum developers, especially in the field of ESP, the book is intended as a theoretical exploration of genre in general and more specifically the characterization of one particular genre: social science research texts.

Although the work at hand is primarily of a descriptive nature, it is of relevance for practitioners in the field of ESP and EAP. Consideration of its use in classrooms leads to the question of the teachability of generic varieties in general. This is a question that has been addressed primarily by first-language researchers, a point to keep in mind in our glimpse at the debate on whether or not generic varieties can be taught. There are many linguists involved in the debate, but we will focus on only two sets of researchers at opposite ends of the cline, who both base their conclusions on work with native speakers of English: Freedman (1993), on the one hand, and Williams and Colomb (1993), on the other, since their work most thoroughly and succinctly summarizes the two positions on the issue. Freedman's position is that it is neither possible nor, even if it were possible, desirable to explicitly teach generic structure to students. Her argument seems to rest on three premises: first, because genres are what she calls, in line with Miller (1994), social actions or rhetorical responses to recurring situations, they are fluid in nature and dynamic, and they therefore cannot be taught because they are always changing in response to different needs. Second, because these responses are always situated in a particular context, generic features cannot be taught outside that context. Finally, she suggests that these two conditions, fluidity and social action, are of primary importance in the characterization of genre and that textual features are secondary to 'rhetorical actions' (which themselves cannot be taught, in her view).

The debate about whether one should teach genres or not seems to rest at least in part on the question of whether the fluidity of the genre is such as to counter the conventionalized features that make up typified rhetorical actions. The fact that they are typified and recognized as genres because of conventionalized features suggests, however, that there is a counterbalancing static nature to genres for extended periods. Furthermore, while the dynamic nature of genres is evident, their conventional character is such that different social institutions and communities can easily identify typical generic features. This would seem to be the view of Williams and Colomb (1993) who, based on their work with a wide range of native speakers of English at different stages of university study, suggest that explicit teaching of salient features of genres is beneficial. They maintain that it is not so much a question of whether 'students get by without explicit teaching, but whether explicit teaching improves their performance to a level of proficiency that repays the cost in time and effort' (p. 255). To support this point, they offer the following quote: explicit teaching has 'clearly positive effects on the *rate* at which learners acquire the language, and probably beneficial effects on their *ultimate level of attainment*' (Larsen-Freeman and Long, 1991: 321). Williams and Colomb (1993) further claim that if teachers embrace only implicit teaching methods and avoid explicitly focusing students' attention on the forms they are learning, then the teachers hide from the students the ideological commitments and consequences of particular generic forms. They suggest that explicit teaching is a necessary step in empowering students to choose how they will participate in the communities they encounter.

What is clear from our brief discussion is that the question needs further exploration based at least in part on clear and systematic descriptions of generic varieties. The current study, then, is important not because its findings can be directly applied to ESP classrooms but because it provides a systematic method of analysis for researchers involved in the study of genre and discourse. In addition, the method can serve as a model for other descriptions so that we can arrive at clear and thorough representations of different varieties of generic types. Furthermore, we would, in agreement with Williams and Colomb, suggest that systematic descriptions of genres such as the one we offer, combined with discussions of the context in which they occur, go a long way towards helping students, particularly L2 learners, understand how to participate more completely in the scientific communities which they are entering. In the words of Berkenkotter and Huckin (1995: 1):

> Genres are the media through which scholars and scientists communicate with their peers. Genres are intimately linked to a discipline's methodology and they package information in ways that conform to a discipline's norms, values, and ideology. Understanding the genres of written communication in one's field is, therefore, essential to professional success.

The search for structure

Progenitors of genre analysis

In order to further situate our own research, we will briefly review work on expository discourse, beginning with Meyer and Rice's (1984) important study that provides a description of text structure in terms of macropropositions – 'the relationships among ideas represented in complexes of propositions or para-graphs' (p. 326). This is a useful proposal for the study of text processing, but does not offer a system that accounts for the structures of these propositions and of those that indicate the author's communicative intent. The text-based model proposed by Meyer and Freedle (1984), however, does capture logical relations at the macrostructure level (which the authors term 'rhetorical relations'). Texts can be organized according to the following relations:

> *description*, in which the collection of attributes relates to the topic, e.g. a news article;
> *collection*, 'a grouping or listing of concepts or ideas by association', e.g. definitions in a textbook, or in more organized form, a historical chronology;
> *causation*, composed of antecedent and consequent;
> *comparison/contrast*;
> *problem/solution* in which 'at least one aspect of the solution matches in content and stops an antecedent of the problem'.

Hoey's studies are also interesting because the model he provides, an expanded problem/solution format (1979; 1983) with the following components, can be applied to both narrative and expository prose:

1. situation
2. aspect of situation requiring a response (i.e. problem)
3. response to aspect of situation requiring a response
4. result of response to aspect of situation requiring a response
5. evaluation of (4)

These studies offer a macro-level analysis of certain expository structures and contribute to the identification of discourse structure of different text types; however, they do not attempt to define a genre.

A closer precursor of genre analysis is found in the early work by Coulthard and Montgomery (1981) on the units that comprise the structure of classroom discourse. However, 'no suggestions were made as to the internal structure in terms of chained constituent elements' (p. 31). Because of this lack, the authors were unable to 'characterize any prospective sequence structure' (p. 31). This led to an inability to predict the types of units that are likely to follow each other, the sequences themselves, and the linguistic features characterizing each of the units in these sequences.

Genre analysis

Other more current studies reflect related problems. Golebiowski (1998) presents data on the rhetorical structure of introductions to research articles in Polish and English. But since the study is contrastive and interested in underlying cultural values, specific linguistic realizations are not systematically developed. Both Bhatia (1993) and Kong (1998) offer useful insights into the rhetorical differences between different kinds of business letters, basing their analyses on Swales' (1990) move structure, with Kong adding rhetorical structure theory (following Mann and Thompson [1988]); however, the systematic realizations of the different rhetorical categories are not provided.

Scientific discourse: from witnessing to constructing reality

When we turn to studies of scientific discourse, the first of two related approaches is Myers, who considers scientific writing a form of narrative. In *Writing Biology* (1990), he examines the process of writing and the ways in which authors are concerned with achieving consensus for their position at different stages of writing. The work illustrates how the authors construct and reinterpret narratives to convince an audience of a perspective and position. This is perhaps most evident when there is a controversy about some scientific point. As Journet (1990: 166–7) points out, authors

> create versions of the texts under debate that differ in some ways from the versions the original authors intended . . . In a controversy, scientists summarize or paraphrase each other's work in ways that tend to further their own positions . . . This is what science is: the competing arrangement of data.

In the second approach to genre studies in scientific writing, and to the social construction of knowledge, Bazerman (1987a) traces the evolution of scientific articles, highlighting the degree to which its rhetorical forms are products of social needs. The work focuses on the examination of how the scientific production of texts evolved in order to negotiate scientific knowledge at differing times and places. Bazerman begins with a study of the first scientific journal in English, *The Philosophical Transactions of the Royal Society of London*, which was founded in 1665 by Henry Oldenburg who

> began to see how increased sharing of information goaded working scientists to produce more and to reveal more of what they were doing . . . From the beginning, [Oldenburg] sensed that science needed to be agonistically structured, so that each player – seeing the moves of the others – makes counter-moves attempting to defend his or her position and to eliminate his or her opponents from the field. (Bazerman, 1987a: 295)

As Bazerman recounts, the *Transactions*, initially a journal for a general audience, gradually became more selective for professional interest and quality. In the middle of the eighteenth century, two innovations were instituted to raise professional standards: referees were introduced and the secretary-editor was replaced by an editorial board which would review and select manuscripts to be published. Bazerman convincingly demonstrates the evolution of journal publication from a position of peripheral interest to the scientist of 1750 to one of primary importance in the twentieth century. Researchers gradually came to recognize that their work meant more for being part of a socially legitimated, critical, socially interactive and cumulative communal process, centred on publication in socially recognized forums. This work was screened by gatekeepers, subjected to public criticism, but, hopefully, ultimately rewarded by being cited by others and accepted into a codified literature:

> an event in nature is not an empirical fact with scientific meaning until it is seen, identified and labeled as having a particular meaning . . . Only by making the fact communal can one claim discovery of that fact for oneself and reap the rewards of it. (Bazerman, 1987a: 302)

Group integration, then, as represented in journal publication, has become so much the hallmark of modern science that Kuhn takes it as the primary indicator of mature science (Bazerman, 1987a: 301). This emphasis on the communal parallels the transition from live demonstration to the recording of events. In the early history of the Royal Society, the scientist would demonstrate what he had found before the assembled members; this demonstration would be recorded in the *Transactions* and verified in writing by witnesses (Swales, 1990). Originally, witnesses were all the members of the Society, but eventually witnessing devolved on a single witness, the researcher. According to Bazerman (1987a), this change meant that persuasion was transformed from public demonstrations of facts to the symbolic representation of events in the published report:

> Thus authority now comes not from one's sources, nor from one's good person, nor even from a publicly witnessed fact, but from a representation of events, hewing closely enough to events and defining the events so carefully so as to answer all critics, seem plausible to readers with extensive knowledge and experience with similar events, and to hold up against future attempts to create similar events. (p. 303)

In fact, some of the ground rules for the scientific report as 'witnessing' were laid down by Robert Boyle in the middle of the seventeenth century. He strove for 'virtual witnessing': the production in a reader's mind of such an image of an experimental scene as obviates the necessity for either its direct witness or its replication (Shapin, cited in Swales, 1990: 111). 'Virtual witnessing' involved the following rhetorical techniques:

1. any illustrations of apparatus in the published work were to be 'realistic, exact, and detailed';
2. accounts of experiments were deliberately elaborate to encourage the reader 'to believe that he was getting a full and honest account';
3. accounts of *failed* experiments were included;
4. philosophical speculation was avoided.

Linguistic choices evolved in conjunction with these rhetorical 'rules'. According to Ard (1983, cited by Swales, 1990) the use of 'I' in early scientific discourse and a prescription against use of the passive voice are related to the central role of the observer at that time.

In another study, Bazerman (1987b) examines the development of experimental psychology, which was the first social science to establish a specialized discourse distinguished from philosophical discourse. This became the model for sociology and for political science, which did not start to develop a predominantly scientific style until the 1920s.

Today, the American Psychological Association *Publication Manual* symbolizes and instrumentally realizes the influence and power of the official style. Whereas the first *Instructions for Manuscripts* (February, 1929) could be expressed in six and a half pages, and were for general guidance only, current editions of the *Manual* offer hundreds of pages of distinctly prescriptive rules, with one section focused almost exclusively on experimental reports. According to Bazerman, this evolution was rooted in the ascendancy of behaviourism in the period between the two world wars, which shaped the rhetorical possibilities. The researcher in experimental psychology was transformed from one who reasons about the mind to a performer of experiments, maker of calculations and presenter of results. 'As behaviorism gradually gained influence, authors began presenting results as ends in themselves, to fill gaps in other results, rather than as potential answers to theoretical questions' (Bazerman, 1987b: 139).

This evolution resulted once again in rhetorical consequences such as:

a. the hypothesis, which usually appeared in the conclusion, now moved up to the opening and became the main unifying element in the article;
b. the 'problem' came to mean the test of the hypothesis and the 'discussion' the confirmation of the hypothesis;
c. articles decreased in scope and length, since their function changed to merely adding bits of information to the literature.

The underlying theme of these accounts is the development of generic varieties in response to changing social needs:

1. The changes are social, primarily motivated by different needs and requirements of society at different periods of history. As Journet (1990: 163) suggests in her review of the work of Bazerman, Gould and Myers, science is now seen to be constructed rather than discovered; it is 'a series of arguments for particular interpretations of data (or even arguments for what constitutes data) rather than the display of self-evident facts'. This focus on socially constructed knowledge led to considerations about the processes of construction, namely writing.
2. The products must reflect previous research of the discourse community, echoing Bakhtin's notion of heteroglossia with different texts responding to past texts and echoing elements of other texts (Bakhtin, 1990).
3. The texts represent a collaborative effort because they are often authored by more than one individual figuratively speaking, as the authors process

their text to conform with the structures of an unseen audience of other scientists. They are more collaborative also in a literal sense because journals prescribe through style manuals, and editors and referees recommend revisions. The final product then, in the words of Knorr-Cetina (1981: 106) 'is a multilayered hybrid co-produced by the authors and by members of the audience to which it is directed'.

In yet another study of the evolution of scientific discourse, Halliday (1988) provides a new perspective on the ways in which the discourse of science has become depersonalized in response to changing societal needs, reflecting a similarly social focus on the nature of the presentation of scientific knowledge. He found that 'as scientific discourse has come to be depersonalized, during the past hundred years or so, personal projections have tended to be increasingly hedged around: '*Smith suggested that* was replaced by *Smith's suggestion was that* . . . while *I suggested that* . . . disappeared almost entirely' (Halliday, 1988: 174). In a similar vein, Hyland (1998) studies the use of hedging in research articles, providing a list of lexical items that realize this concept. Hyland demonstrates how hedging is used in scientific writing to negotiate knowledge claims and to accommodate to the conventions of the scientific community.

The social context

The evolution of purpose and associated changing rhetorical features in response to changing societal norms requires considerations of context. The question of context is of course not new, originating in the early work of Malinowski, who insisted on the necessity of recognizing two types of context: context of culture and context of situation. The former pertains to the broader context of culture, which engenders a wide range of behaviours, and the latter to the particular situation to which a particular linguistic behaviour responds. Interestingly, Malinowski originally thought that 'context of situation' was irrelevant for scientific writing.

> I opposed civilized and scientific to primitive speech, and argued as if the theoretical uses of words in modern philosophic and scientific writing were completely detached from their pragmatic sources. This was an error . . . Between the savage use of words and the most abstract and theoretical one there is only a difference of degree. Ultimately all the meaning of all words is derived from bodily experience. (1935, vol. 2: 58, quoted in Halliday and Hasan, 1985)

These insights were extended into a linguistic model by Firth and then Halliday and other systemic functional linguists. The concept of context among these linguists centres on three situational constructs: field, tenor and mode, which compose register. To review interpretations of registerial constructs chronologically, we begin with one of the early definitions of register by Gregory and Carroll (1978: 64), who maintain that register is a 'useful abstraction linking variations of language to variations of social context'. Halliday and Hasan

(1976: 23) provide further specifications, defining register as 'the set of meanings, the configuration of semantic patterns, that are typically drawn upon under the specified conditions, along with the words and structures that are used in the realization of these meanings'. Later, Halliday amended this slightly to suggest that a register 'is the configuration of semantic resources that the member of the culture associates with a situation type.' 'It is the meaning potential that is accessible in a given social context' (cited in Martin, 1992: 498). In recent versions of these constructs (Gregory, 1988; Halliday and Hasan, 1985; Martin, 1992), then, it is generally accepted that field refers to the social event that the text is helping to realize; tenor, to the type of social relations which obtain between senders and receivers of the text; and mode, to the type of text, especially in terms of the channel (spoken or written) and its rhetorical mode – such as narrative, didactic or persuasive.

Registers arise from those linguistic choices that represent the convergence of values for the contextual systems that impinge upon the text: field, tenor and mode. For example, a first year university lecture in Biology combines choices from that particular field of activity, Biology, with the ways in which lectures are carried out in different geographical and temporal situations. The lecture also activates choices engendered by the tenor of the discourse, determined by the relationship between a lecturer and the audience of, say, first-year students. The lecture is further identifiable by the mode of discourse; in many North American universities, for example, the mode is that of semi-spontaneous speech. (See Gregory and Carroll [1978] and Leckie-Tarry [1995] for a more complete discussion of the registerial constructs.) Each of these constructs in turn influences linguistic choices, a lecture employing certain features unique to it and vastly different from those of recipes, for example. In Halliday's (1978: 122) terms, 'The field, tenor, and mode act collectively as determinants of the text through their specification of the register; at the same time they are systematically associated with the linguistic system through the functional components of the semantics'.

Applying these contextual constructs to scientific research texts offers a way of examining and pinpointing the converging values of a variety of context types and of predicting features of each. As Halliday suggested, 'The notion of register is thus a form of prediction; given that we know the situation, the social context of language use, we can predict a great deal about the language that will occur, with reasonable probability of being right' (Halliday, 1978, cited in Gregory, 1988: 315).

To illustrate this, notes on the role of contextual constructs on scientific research articles might include the following:

1. **Field**: accounts for the institutionalized forum for exchange of ideas among scholars and includes 'extending, transmitting or exploring knowledge' (Halliday, 1988). It also includes purposes such as: sharing one's discovery with peers; making one's claim to a new theory or discovery, or bidding for credit for testing a specific hypothesis or challenging an existing claim, thereby justifying a greater allocation of social

rewards; providing background information for specialists, present and future.

2. **Tenor**: accounts for the relationships between authors and readers. The author is expected to address readers as peers; the author should not appear personally familiar with readers, i.e. maximal social distance will apply; social norms require objectivity, modesty, credit to one's colleagues; the audience is expected to be an educated stratum of society; the relative expertise of the author *vis-à-vis* the audience varies (specialist to specialist or specialist to non-specialist, or novice to veterans); the author is addressing a limited audience who might read the text immediately or many years later. Related to these considerations of tenor are ones that Couture (1985) outlines at further delicacy in her discussion of different levels of intrusion. She hypothesizes that each rhetorical section of a research paper reflects the range of the speaker's involvement 'from neutral to fully participatory in the roles of observer of a situation, intruder in social concourse [sic] and manipulator of text' (p. 76). This became evident after we analysed how authors present their results, avoiding explicit expressions of their opinion and submerging their presence. On the other hand, we found that authors are more evaluative in the 'recommendations' section of a research text and try to convince the audience of their perspective.

3. **Mode**: accounts for the choices between written and spoken discourse, among other issues of channel of communication (in the present case, the mode is written discourse). It may be a professional-journal article or a first-person report in which the narrator is the principal participant. It contains features common to both didactic and persuasive prose; the title must be amenable to an abstracting system; the text is performative in that it establishes a claim to 'ownership' of ideas; the text is a report of objective facts (the description of research acts) and an interpretation of those facts; the code is preferably English even when it is not the author's native language (documented by Swales, 1990); the text can be understood as an independent unit but it must be related to past texts and have potential as a progenitor of new texts; some constraints are imposed by the medium (journal): length, certain forms (e.g. form of citations), and revisions indicated by referees.

The necessity of making texts respond to past texts and future ones echoes Bakhtin's (1990: 356) heteroglossia in his discussions of 'language in its historical life and in its relation to other texts'. As he puts it, 'language is something that is historically real, a process of heteroglot development, a process teeming with future and former languages' (1990: 356–7). He continues: 'Language is not a neutral medium that passes freely and easily into the private property of the speaker's intentions; it is populated – overpopulated – with the intentions of others' (1990: 294). Bakhtin's words seem even more relevant to research texts, in which response to previous texts is a necessary component of the genre.

Genre defined

Having briefly discussed the evolution of the research genre and the concept of register, we need to examine the definition of genre itself in order to distinguish it from registerial constructs, with which it is frequently conflated. The notion of genre has undergone a metamorphosis in recent years. According to Freedman and Medway (1994: 1): 'Traditional definitions of genre focused on textual regularities. In traditional literary studies the genres ... were defined by conventions of form'. More recently, however, in composition studies and current studies of rhetoric the conceptions of genre have expanded 'to be able to connect a recognition of regularities in discourse types with a broader social and cultural understanding of language in use' (p. 1). The focus has come to be on ways to 'unpack the complex social, cultural, institutional and disciplinary factors at play in the production of specific kinds of writing' (p. 2). Particular attention then is paid to the purpose that different genres achieve in particular social situations.

For linguists such as Ventola and Martin, the focus is similar: 'the classification of social interactions or social processes into types' (Ventola, 1989: 129). Genres range from poems and narratives to newspaper editorials, eulogies, scientific papers, and research articles. Martin's (1985: 250) emphasis, in his definition of genre, is equally social, maintaining that genres are:

> how things get done, when language is used to accomplish them ... The term genre is used ... to embrace each of the linguistically realized activities which comprise so much of our culture ... [Genre] represents at an abstract level the verbal strategies used to accomplish social purposes of many kinds. (Martin, 1985: 250)

Swales (1990) also categorizes genres according to their set of shared communicative purposes, offering an extensive elaboration of the concept. Thus, letters do not comprise a genre but letters for certain purposes do, e.g. a request for a paper. Neither are genres defined by shared content or by common interlocutors. The purposes of each genre are recognized by the expert members of the parent discourse community, and thereby constitute the rationale for the genre. Swales' research and references also make explicit other relevant components of genre:

1. 'A genre is a group of acts unified by a constellation of forms that recurs in each of its members. These forms, *in isolation*, appear in other discourses. What is distinctive about the acts in a genre is a recurrence of the forms *together* in constellation.' (Campbell and Jamieson, 1978: 20, quoted in Swales, 1990: 43)
2. A genre is a class of communicative events, that is, events in which language (and/or paralanguage) plays both a significant and an indispensable role.
3. Instances of genres vary in their prototypicality.

This last point has been extended by Paltridge (1997). In discussing the origins and aspects of prototype theory according to Wittgenstein and Rosch, Paltridge maintains that:

> people categorize objects according to a prototypical image they build in their mind of what it is that represents the object in question . . . People are shown to categorize in relation to prototypes which have a common core at the centre and fade off at the edges. (p. 53)

Paltridge draws an analogy to genre in line with prototype theory, maintaining that 'the closer the representation of a genre is to the prototypical image of the genre, the clearer an example it will be as an instance of that particular genre' (p. 394).

4. 'The rationale behind a genre establishes constraints on allowable contributions in terms of their content, positioning and form.' (Swales, 1990: 52) In terms of the present research, for example, the fact that the rationale of a research article is to present one's (positive) results constrains presenting discarded hypotheses.

Issues in genre analysis

Swales' list of defining characteristics (above) is the most comprehensive in the literature. But even with such an extensive treatment, there is a significant problem from our perspective in that he offers no linguistic criteria to determine that text A and text B are members of the same genre. This problem is similar to the one referred to earlier in the work of Coulthard and Montgomery (1981) on moves in classroom discourse. They did not identify linguistic features, and this, as we have suggested, leads to an inability to 'characterize any prospective sequence structure' as they themselves say (p. 31). This is a serious failing, especially if the intention is a complete description of a generic variety.

Another area of concern in genre studies has to do with the conflation of register and genre, which is apparent in several analyses. First, the aspect of rhetorical purpose, which underlies definitions of genre, has been variously conflated with differing constructs of register. Halliday (1965) considers rhetorical purpose as field, a matter of register, but later (Halliday and Hasan, 1985) includes in mode, another situational factor, the purpose of the text in terms of categories such as persuasive, expository and didactic. Gregory originally (1967) included didactic within functional tenor, while Fawcett (1980) categorized purpose as a separate contextual variable in its own right. Gregory, however, has come to view functional tenor or purpose at a deeper level, underlying a discourse, generating the discourse itself, coming closer to the perspective of Fawcett on this. (For a fuller discussion, see Martin, 1992: 501.)

Hasan, approaching the question from another perspective, suggests that in examining the source of generic structures, the values of field, mode and tenor (the components of the contextual configuration) are responsible for the total range of textual structures available within a genre. In other words, genre is the expression of the contextual configuration. When these values are common to a class of social events, the texts will resemble one another functionally and can be categorized as belonging to the same genre (Hasan, 1977, cited in Ventola, 1987: 43).

Thus, different social situations will produce different genres because each social situation has its own configuration of values. To the extent that different social contexts share values, structural elements will be shared. Once again, the conflation of genre and register is evident; other related areas of concern surface in the following discussion.

Ventola (1987) and Martin (1992) consider genre as a semiotic level in its own right, where the ways in which social acts are accomplished can be captured within a particular culture. *Semiotic* refers to a system of signs that have meaning for a particular culture. Culture is composed of many semiotic systems, with language, kinds of dress and music among them. The semiotic organization of our social system may be a system corresponding to the linguistic system; when we know the values from the semiotic variables of the social context, we can predict types of meaning choices that will be selected from the linguistic system (Halliday, 1978; Ventola, 1984). Thus, 'genre must be seen as a semiotic system which makes its own meanings in terms of generic structures in texts' (Ventola, 1987: 77).

Martin (1992) distinguishes between register and genre by maintaining that register is a semiotic system in its own right, constituted by the contextual variables of field, mode and tenor, whereas Halliday uses the term 'register' simply to refer to language as context's expression plane. Furthermore, Martin (1992: 495) postulates the relationship between genre and register as 'two communication planes, genre (context of culture) and register (context of situation), with register functioning as the expression form of genre, at the same time as language functions as the expression form of register'.

This statement entails that genre and register have no internal constituents. In Hjelmslevian terms, they are denotative semiotic systems compared to language, which is therefore a 'connotative' system (Ventola, 1987: 57). Although drawing upon register for its expression, genres constrain the ways in which register variables of field, tenor and mode can be combined in a particular society. Thus, three separate semiotic planes are interdependent: 'Register can then itself be organised with respect to field, tenor, and mode, reflecting metafunctional diversity in its expression form, leaving genre to concentrate on the integration of meanings engendered by field, tenor, and mode as systemically related social processes' (Martin, 1992: 495).

While register and genre in Martin and Ventola's explanations have been clearly delineated as separate strata, problems remain. The claim that generic structures are realized by register seems at variance with holding that generic structures are a separate semiotic system. A suggestion more consistent with the definitions of genre presented above would be that generic structures are drawn from a different order of constituents, which form a system defined in terms of communicative activity, e.g. offering greetings, apologies, making an appointment. Furthermore, the generic system allows for non-verbal realization of certain structures so that to place language as the ultimate realization of genre seems inaccurate.

It is evident from this discussion of the overlap between registerial and genre constructs that we need to outline criteria by which we can more definitively identify the two. One of the clearest characterizations of each and ways in which they can be so distinguished is that offered by Couture (1986). Refuting the idea that a particular register realizes a particular genre, she suggests instead that they represent two different organizations. Registers constrain choices at the linguistic level (vocabulary and syntax), whereas genre constrains choices at the level of discourse structure. Further, genres 'can only be realized in completed texts or texts that can be projected as complete, for a genre does more than specify kinds of codes extant in a group of related texts; it specifies conditions for beginning, continuing and ending a text' (Couture, 1986, as quoted in Swales, 1990: 41), although, as Ventola (1987) argues (below), not all these constraints need be observed for a genre to remain identifiable. Genres such as research reports or business reports, Couture goes on to explain, 'are completable structured texts, while registers (language of scientific reporting, language of newspaper reporting) ... represent more generalizable stylistic choices' (p. 41). Ideally, genre A is written in its complementary register A. A lecture and a journal report on the same subject might share a register but not generic structures. At the other extreme, naive writers sometimes combine the structures for one genre, e.g. scientific research report, and the register for another, which is one of the major problems for second language learners trying to produce writing that is appropriate to a particular genre.

In Couture's (1985) study of student writing quality, she identifies the problem revolving around registerial and genre choices. She suggests that 'high-quality compositions develop a theme through consistent choices within a single register and a single genre. Less successful student compositions fail to express a consistent register or genre' (p. 81). In examining a student composition (see below, Sample A) that received low ratings from three readers, Couture identifies the main problem as one of 'discontinuous semantic functions', going on to say that, 'The writer attempts a register one could call the language of "casual observation" and approximates the genre of the "personal essay"' (p. 83).

Sample A
There are many people in this world that has a good sense of humour. Having a good sense of humour is something that you have to develop. There are people that can joke about anything that maybe troubling them. They are the kind of people that can make a long boring Monday at Wayne State a short cheerful day. Everybody that work with me has this kind of sense of humour. The hospital that I work at is having trouble with their budget. Because of this they have what they call a hiring freeze. This mean that if somebody get fire or quit they are not going to hire anyone. To do the work it requires four people. Because one girl quit there is only three people to do this job. Instead of complaining we sit and make make [sic] about who is going to do the extra work. Sometime we say that superwoman

and superman is going to do the work. To keep our mind off the extra (work) we crack jokes about each other.

But like other places there are some people that can't take a joke. You can always tell who these people are because they don't have many friend. They get mad if you say something about them. (Couture, 1985: 83)

Yet another approach to the problem of classifying genre is outlined by Hasan and Ventola. Based on a corpus of service encounters (dialogues between customers and shop attendants), Hasan offers the first conceptual model for classifying texts according to genres, referred to as the 'Generic Structure Potential' (Halliday and Hasan, 1985). The GSP specifies the obligatory (genre defining) and typical optional elements of the genre and their canonical ordering. These elements in their normal order are to be used as criteria for determining whether texts are complete or incomplete. For instance, the exchange of greetings and casual conversation between a visitor to a shop and a salesperson cannot be classified as a 'service encounter' if an inquiry about goods to be purchased is not realized.

An alternative to Hasan's model is offered by Martin (originally 1985) and applied to a corpus of texts by Ventola (1987, 1989). Martin and Ventola present a more flexible system of genre realization, which allows for otherwise deficient texts (i.e. missing some obligatory elements) to be nevertheless recognizable as within the genre. Martin's innovation is the development of generic system networks 'formulated on the basis of similarities and differences between text structures which thereby define text types' (Martin 1992: 505). These networks capture the array of features from which genre (and also register) choices are made within a continuum of increasingly delicate options. The selection of particular features is realized by a particular generic structure element. The networks graphically demonstrate the interrelationship of genres ('agnateness' in Martin's terminology). Similar contextual features lead to the realization of similar activities. For example, the feature 'unappointed' common to visits to a travel agency and to a shop necessitates the instantiation of 'service bid'. A difference in features gives rise to one or more different generic structures, e.g. [demand for] goods is expressed by 'pay' + 'goods handover', which are absent when the feature [demand for] information is selected (Ventola, 1987: 65). Since Martin has stipulated that genre, not register, variables are responsible for generating schematic structure, a model based upon genre agnateness can override register variations arising from field, mode or tenor values. Thus, in the Martin/Ventola view, service encounters in a post office, a shop or a travel agency are variations on one basic genre.

Figure 1.1 represents our adaptation of the agnation network, for scientific research reports, showing how genres and subgenres are realized from a selection of features at increasing levels of delicacy. In our representation, the feature [greetings], for example, would not be chosen in a written report, while [review of literature] would usually not be realized in talk at a conference.

Ventola (1987), however, suggests that the networks do not specify sequence of structures; second, they lead to the assumption that the selection of certain features has an inevitable specific generic realization. In short, a network offers

Figure 1.1 A suggested agnation network for scientific research reports

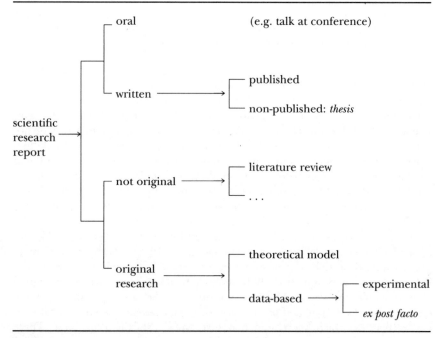

Realizations:
Scientific research report → + explanation of problem
                              + explanation of attempted solution
                              + evaluation
Oral   → + greetings (personal narrative)
Written   → + review of previous literature
Original research   → + report of present author's contribution
Data-based   → + results
Experimental   → + description of controls

a static, synoptic view at an abstract level. To account for the dynamic nature of text production, Ventola (1987: 67) proposes a flowchart which 'captures how in individual texts the synoptic view of genre can be "manipulated" to generate structurally unique texts which nevertheless belong to the same genre'. The flowchart obviates the need to define genres in terms of obligatory elements because the flowchart representation shows how the realization process of a text may bypass practically any obligatory element. 'The membership of a text in a particular genre is thus defined in terms of the shared linguistic and non-linguistic realizations generated by a genre-specific flowchart . . .' (p. 77).

At first glance, it would appear that flowcharts are applicable only to texts involving more than one creator, where A and B influence each other's choices. However, text creation by one person can also be represented by flowcharts. The author can be said to interact with the schema of a text to create her own product. Broadly speaking, a generic structure may be likened to the course of a river; the riverbed directs the stream but is also modified by the flow. In research texts, for example, certain features of the context/situation (e.g. whether the results of the research are satisfactory) constrain the choice of an element. As these choices are made, they constrain subsequent choices of elements.

To summarize what we have been glimpsing thus far, the major contributions of Martin (1992) and Ventola (1987) are: 1) distinguishing genre from register as semiotic planes; 2) relegating the representation of field, mode and tenor to register, rather than to generic structures; and 3) developing criteria through which individual texts can be evaluated for membership in a particular genre. Applying this model to a genre of oral discourse, Ventola has shown how text unfolds dynamically and how specific networks for context variables can predict the range of choices available to interlocutors. The result is a rigorous method for analysing oral discourse between two interlocutors.

While Ventola's analysis shows the impact of the immediate situation (e.g. whether stamps or travel plans are being discussed), her analysis stops short of embedding this social process in its cultural context. How are particular social norms reflected in the choice of and realizations of generic structures? Moreover, what variations can be created when individual 'authors' interact with the typical generic structures?

Rhetorical functions in research texts

Questions of another sort in the literature focus on the nature of rhetorical structure in relation to genre. For the purpose of our study and discussion we consider structure in written texts in terms of *rhetorical functions*, which are defined by their communicative purpose. This is in line with Miller's view of genre, cited above, as representing 'a typified social action' (Miller, 1994: 24).

In terms of our study, the primary rhetorical functions in reports of empirical scientific research are:

   I. Motivating the research (form = Introduction section)
  II. Describing the collection of the data (form = Methods section)
 III. Reporting the results (form = Results section)
 IV. Evaluating the results (form = Discussion section)

These primary functions are well known, but the study of the secondary functions ('moves' for Swales [1981] and subsequent literature) within these divisions is an ongoing consideration for genre analysts.

According to the extensive review of the literature on research articles provided by Swales (1990), the earliest examination of rhetorical structure was in 1979; Swales' own study in 1981 (revised in 1990) continues to be the hallmark for genre analysis of Introductions. Subsequent analyses have concentrated on Discussion sections (rather than Introductions) in various academic fields.

The problems with these, however, centre around the types and number of structures identified, which vary greatly, with three found by Nwogu (1997); five offered by Gnutzmann and Oldenburg (1991), and by Lewin and Fine (1996); six by McKinlay (1982); seven by Belanger (1982); eight by Dubois (1997) and by Holmes (1997); eleven by Hopkins and Dudley-Evans (1988), and by Peng (1987). Only one move, summarizing results, is common to the last five named studies. These studies contribute significantly to the field of ESP but leave certain methodological problems that centre, first, on the fact that criteria for the linguistic realization of generic elements (moves) have been overlooked or not rigidly defined. Second, there is a diversity of views on determining the extent of each move.

Although the basic moves for both service encounters and research texts have been proposed, realizational criteria for each move have not been provided. Instead of these criteria, the concept of semantic properties has been used to categorize specific moves. But this concept itself has been subject to different interpretations. For example, for Hasan (Halliday and Hasan, 1985) the element 'service request' in service encounters is realized by demand, reference to goods, and quantity of goods. In contrast, although presumably based on Hasan's model, Samraj (1989) lists as 'semantic attributes' classes which can be considered speech acts or rhetorical functions, e.g. 'Focusing on object', 'Labelling' and 'Descriptions'. For Martin and Ventola, the analysis stops at the structural level; the 'language stratum' (Ventola, 1987) specifications in terms of lexico-grammatical realization are not a substantial part of the analysis.

Similarly, analysis of the research genre lacks uniform standards for move identification. Swales (1990) appears to combine criteria from different systems. For instance, he distinguishes Move 2 ('establishing the research niche') by either lexicogrammatical criteria, such as negation in the determiner, or by rhetorical function such as 'logical conclusions'. Dubois (1997) offers criteria for distinguishing only two of the twenty rhetorical functions in her classification system. Dudley-Evans identifies moves by lexicogrammatical signals. For Discussion texts, he (1986, 1994) relies on specific lexical signals. (For example, the lexical items 'an examination' or 'revealed' are evidence of the report of a finding.) But he finds that lexical clues are not always effective. This deficiency necessitates consultation with specialist informants and comparison to the analysis produced by other approaches, such as clause relations. Evident is the lack of an objective method for identifying specific moves; minimal realizational criteria have not been provided for the genres reported on in the literature.

Another problem concerns the extent of a move and is evident in Swales' own study (1990) and those cited by him and by Dubois (1997). The extent of a 'move' differs between analyses of introduction sections and those of discussion sections with the former operating at a much higher level of generalization. Thus, Swales' (1990) classic three-move introduction sequence is: 'establish a territory', 'establish a niche', and 'occupy the niche'. In contrast, analysts of discussion sections specify functions such as 'statement of results', 'explanation' and 'hypothesis'.

The wide variation in delineating the extent of a move may be attributable to the use of two different units of analysis. The approach of Swales (1981,

1990) is the most consistent since he considers moves as discourse units rather than lexicogrammatical units. However, he does not address the question of how move boundaries can be determined. In dealing with this difficult problem, others have tried to align move boundaries with lexicogrammatical units. In analysing introductions, Crookes (1986) used the sentence as his basic unit of coding. As a result, Crookes' raters disagreed on the coding of complex sentences in which each clause realized a different function, such as 'Although fluorescent antibody studies have established . . . , the form and detailed arrangement of myosin has remained a mystery' (p. 66).

Inconsistencies also emerge in the analysis of discussion sections. For example, Hopkins and Dudley-Evans (1988) define moves in terms of function only. Although Dubois (1997) adds a lexicogrammatical variable, with each independent clause coded for rhetorical function, the difficulty is that this unit was not coterminous with a move; independent clauses often realized more than one move.

If an appropriate lexicogrammatical unit were found, the question would arise, 'Should the occurrence of each such unit be considered a separate rhetorical move?' To those authors who define a move grammatically, five contiguous sentences expressing, for example, 'conclusions', presumably are coded as five moves, whereas those who classify moves semantically (e.g. Swales, 1990) would consider any number of contiguous clauses performing the same function as one move.

Thus, the fact that various writers have found different numbers and types of moves may not be due to the differences in the scientific field studied (e.g. agriculture vs. biology) but due to the differences in methods used to measure 'moves'. (See Table 1.1, which compares the methods of four important introduction and discussion analyses.)

Within the Discussion section alone, analyses are also quite varied. One result, as noted by Dubois (1997), is a difference in level of generality among moves. This difference can be seen from a comparison of classifications in five studies (Table 1.2), which will be discussed in more detail in Chapter 4. Among them, Holmes (1997) is the only study of 'social science' texts. However, the academic fields he chose were different from ours (history, political science and sociology), whereas we obtained our corpus from the fields of psychology and

Table 1.1 'Move' classifications in scientific research articles, in four studies

Author	Year	Text	Coding system	Field
Crookes	1986	introduction	sentence	mixed
Hopkins and Dudley-Evans	1988	discussion	lexicogrammatical	agriculture
Swales	1990	introduction	semantic	mixed
Dubois	1997	discussion	independent clause	biomedicine

Table 1.2 Comparison of 'moves' in Discussion sections as determined by five previous studies

Move	Author				
	B	H	P	D	RH
1. Introduction	✓	–	–	–	–
Background information	–	✓	✓	–	✓
Common knowledge	–	–	–	r	–
2. Summary of results	✓	✓	✓	r	✓
3. Conclusions, deduction	✓	✓	✓	r	–
4. What results suggest	✓	–	–	–	–
5. Further questions	✓	–	–	–	–
6. Possible answers to future questions	✓	–	–	–	–
7. (Un)expected outcome*	–	✓	✓	–	✓
8. Reference to previous research	✓	✓	–	r	✓
9. Explanation of unsatisfactory result	–	✓	–	–	✓
10. Exemplification*	–	✓	–	–	–
11. Hypothesis*	–	✓	✓	r	–
12. Recommendation*	–	✓	✓	–	✓
13. Justification*	–	✓	✓	–	–
14. Observation	–	–	✓	–	–
15. Comparison	–	–	✓	–	–
16. Validation	–	–	✓	–	–
17. Metatext	–	–	–	r	–
18. Explanation	–	–	✓	–	–
19. Methodology	–	–	–	r	–
20. Comment*	–	–	–	r	–
21. Developments*	–	–	–	–	✓

Key
B   = Belanger, Neuroscience, 1982, cited in Dubois, 1997
H   = Hopkins and Dudley-Evans, Biology and Agriculture, 1988
P   = Peng, Chemical Engineering, 1987, cited in Dubois, 1997
D   = Dubois, Biomedicine, 1997
RH = Holmes, Social Science and History, 1997
✓   = considered a 'move'
r   = Considered a 'rhetorical function'
*   **Definitions**
 7. = remarks on whether the result is expected or not
10. = an example to support the author's explanation
11. = a more general claim arising from the experimental results
12. = suggestions for future work
13. = justification of recommendations for future research
20. = the author's evaluation or judgement
21. = outlining parallel or subsequent developments

sociology. His analysis, based on Hopkins and Dudley-Evans (1988), poses the same problems of methodology as do the other studies.

Thus, genre analysis of research texts in the tradition of ESP specialists such as Swales and Dudley-Evans reveals, firstly, inconsistencies in terms of levels of generality and, secondly, no clear criteria for the identification of moves, alternating between lexicogrammatical and semantic criteria without clarifying the reason for this choice. While genre analysts working in the Systemic model have provided more precise tools for analysis, they usually are not concerned with realizational criteria for a *specific* genre.

Summary

We have focused on a variety of approaches to genre analysis and presented the contributions that each makes to the field, as well as the gaps in the studies of generic structure. It is these gaps that we hope to fill in the current work. What we propose is to draw on and adapt approaches that we have discussed to provide a more consistent study of social science research articles with the following principles guiding our study:

1. The prerequisite for the membership of specific texts in a common genre is a shared communicative purpose (Swales, 1990).
2. Within a specific genre, communicative activity defines a system of constituents, which provides the primary structures. Registers are a complementary system that selects the linguistic realization for a particular activity. To give the simplest example, the structure 'greetings' can be realized by a variety of registers: 'Good morning; hello; hi'.
3. Membership of texts in the same genre is established not by a fixed set of obligatory features but by the fact that they select their structural elements from a common repertoire and that these elements tend to form a highly probable pattern (Martin, 1985, 1992; Ventola, 1987, 1988, 1989).
4. While ideal or model texts contain all prototypical elements in canonical sequence, real texts represent an array of possible combinations of prototypical structures. As Ventola (1987) in particular has shown, the process of composing texts 'in the real world' can involve bypassing of certain features, unlimited possibilities for recursions, and even embedding of alien genres within the one being composed.
5. A text is composed of several interdependent strata of structures that generate meanings (Halliday, 1978; Halliday and Hasan, 1985; Hasan, 1984; Martin, 1985; 1992; Ventola, 1987, 1988, 1989).
6. A theory of text must recognize that texts are an outgrowth of social realities encompassing particular social norms and values (acknowledging that even within social constraints, individuals have a continuum of options, which allows them to express their personal messages).

   In sum, to reflect this set of principles, our work is designed:
   a. to provide a rigorous method for determining units of analysis so that

future analyses of the genre of research texts can be related to a common working model;

b. to furnish the rhetorical structures (elements defined by their communicative purposes) that characterize introduction and discussion sections of research articles in social science journals as belonging to a common genre (or two subgenres within the genre 'research article');

c. to provide an objective system of realizations in terms of semantic features. These features are depicted in system networks that show the array of features that represent the choices available within a given context;

d. to demonstrate the flexibility that occurs in real texts by means of a flowchart, which allows for a separate decision-making step at each node in the network, instead of an obligatory sequence;

e. to describe text in terms of several types of constituent strata. Our primary interest is in defining types and components of generic structures. We also examine the boundary-marking system that distinguishes them. Secondly, we incorporate two of the discourse systems that create a cohesive text from these various rhetorical structures: lexical cohesion and reference (participant identification system) (Martin, 1992). The present analysis seeks to describe these discourse systems and to determine if they are sensitive to generic structures;

f. within the bounds of linguistic theory, to embed the research genre within a cultural context, demonstrating its contingency upon social processes and constraints and showing the individual variations within these constraints.

2 Methods

Introduction

The need for analysis and identification of components of different genres is clear, especially since Dubois (1997), in her review of books designed to teach professional writing, found that none clearly spells out the rhetorical work that is expected in different sections (especially Discussions sections of research papers).

However, as we demonstrated in Chapter 1, genre analysis as a field does not systematically provide realization criteria for the structures it proposes; in the genre analysis of research texts, particular problems concerning the number and extent of moves surface. In Swales' (1990) work on genre analysis, he established three generic structures in Introductions, while Gnutzmann and Oldenburg (1991) found four. In Discussions, the number of structures varies greatly, from three offered by Nwogu (1997), to eleven by Peng (1987). In his analysis of Results sections of sociology articles, Brett (1994) found that some structures were unique to Results, while others overlapped with those found in Discussions. While these generic structures are defined by their communicative function (see below), they are referred to as 'moves' by the majority of authors, 'text part segments' by Gnutzmann and Oldenburg (1991) and 'communicative categories' by Brett (1994). This body of work, including the extensive and thorough study of Swales, still leaves two significant problems to be solved. First, Swales' methods (and consequently, those studies based upon his methods) do not specify the extent of a move, giving equal weight to macro and micro rhetorical functions. This leads to inconsistency, particularly evident in Swales' texts where one move variously realizes one rhetorical function or several such functions. The second problem is that no author offers criteria for realizing the rhetorical structures (or moves, as we and others refer to them), and therefore they cannot be independently identified. Because of these problems, analysts cannot make comparisons between texts in different academic fields (e.g. astronomy vs. zoology) or in different modes (dissertation vs. journal article).

In addition to the methodological problems, there has been no focus on the social sciences in previous literature, that is, on fields which specialize in the parameters of human behaviour. Although Swales (1990) included social sciences in his analysis of Introductions, he does not draw conclusions according to academic field. Analyses of Discussion sections that we referred to earlier are based on physical science texts; a recent exception is Holmes (1997), who based his study on texts in sociology, political science and history. The inclusion of history in the 'social sciences' is questionable; see the definition of scientific, below. Therefore, a real need exists to build on and complement the work already done with studies in social science. A second impetus for our work is to develop a standardized method for genre analysis for research texts in any discipline. To begin, we will focus in this chapter on identifying and defining the relevant concepts involved and discussing problems and possible solutions in genre analysis. In Chapters 3 and 4, we will suggest the specific structures relevant to social science research texts.

Definition of concepts

First of all, in our study, a *research text* is a report of empirical, quantitative research, i.e. a data-based report of either an experiment or an *ex post facto* study, testing hypotheses or answering research questions. The *sine qua non* of a research text is its division into sections detailing the background of the study, the methods, the results, and the interpretation of the results. Our analysis is restricted to research texts so defined.

To recall (Chapter 1), we based our definition of genre on Martin's succinct statement (1985: 250) 'genre is how we get things done when language is used to accomplish them' and Swales' (1990) claim that the criterion for classifying certain events as a 'genre' is a set of shared communicative purposes. In other words, genre identification rests solely on communicative purpose, a criterion that has been well established by Searle (1969) who classified disparate realizations according to the speaker's intent.

In scientific texts, these communicative purposes distinguish genres, which are recognized by the expert members of the discourse community – scientists all over the world regardless of the individual cultures to which they belong. We propose to combine Martin's and Swales' approaches so that we can capture the concept of genre as representing the recognized pattern of verbal structures which constitute a social exchange for a specific purpose; these 'verbal structures' comprise in written scientific texts the many 'rhetorical functions' that such texts have to perform.

Furthermore, what is also needed in the specification of genres is the identification of the prototypical elements involved in a particular social event, their sequencing, and the constraints on their realization. A necessary component is a system for the realization of each element. (A fuller discussion of the issues is presented in Chapter 1.) For a review of additional questions of genre analysis, see Ventola (1987).

Corpus

In order to achieve some consistency in our description of the genre, we adopted the following definitions. *Scientific* conforms to Kerlinger's (1973: 11) definition, with a minor change added, in brackets: 'Scientific research is systematic, controlled, empirical and critical investigation of hypothetical propositions about the presumed relations among natural [or social and behavioural] phenomena'.

A *research text*, in this study, therefore, is a report of empirical, quantitative research, i.e. a data-based report of either an experiment or an *ex post facto* study, testing hypotheses or answering research questions.[1] The term *social science* is used in order to be consistent with Crookes (1986) and subsequent literature. We selected only 12 texts so that they could be intensively examined and an integrated depiction of all the systems could be simultaneously provided. We followed in this sense Ventola's work (1987) in which she limited the size of corpus for similar purposes. (The list comprising the sources for texts is provided in the Bibliography.) We have focused on Introductions and Discussions because these sections require substantial rhetorical work of authors and as such illustrate in particular interpersonal considerations, which are a focus of this work.

We further restricted our study to that of valued journals (those most often cited) in preference to a random selection of all journals, since one of our goals was to develop a set of guidelines for students to facilitate their integration into the discourse community of social science. They can accomplish this most easily and quickly by becoming familiar with the most widely read and accepted journals.

Method

To develop a consistent method of analysis, we addressed the following questions which we will deal with in detail below:

- What are the relevant elements in genre analysis?
- What is the unit of analysis?
- How can we identify elements from different texts as instantiations of the same communicative purpose?
- How can we determine the boundaries of a specific element?

We have identified and defined the elements within research texts on the basis of their communicative purposes, those which combine to fulfil the overall purpose of the genre. This decision derives from the fact that these are the most consistent elements in all samples. Perhaps the most problematic outcome of neglecting communicative purpose as a criterion of moves in previous research has been the classification of 'reference to literature' as a separate move. The assumption that 'reference' in itself conveys communicative intent, in the same way that the other rhetorical functions do, seems ill-advised. While Swales (1990) no longer categorizes literature references as a separate move, his original (1981) position influenced subsequent studies (e.g. Crookes, 1986).

Moreover, the term 'references to literature' obscures two distinctions. First, 'references' do not necessarily co-occur with formal citations, as in sentence 3 below. Second, a reference may be expressed non-syntactically within parentheses or expressed only in a list of references at the end of the article. Such relegation of references to secondary status suggests that the author is more interested in highlighting the proposition itself rather than the fact that it has appeared in the literature. In the following examples, we can see that the term 'references to literature' covers various forms as well as a range of differences in communicative intent. References can be non-syntactic (sentence 1 below) or syntactic (sentences 2 and 3 below). At the same time, they may (sentence 1) or may not (sentence 3) cite specific literature. It seems reasonable to assume that these different practices reflect different intentions.

1. 'This formulation [hypothesis of authors] is supported by the evidence that the specific quality of thought disorder ... differs between schizophrenic and manic patients (Names, 1985)' (Text 4) [**non-syntactic reference, with specific citation, intent is to support authors' interpretation**]
2. 'Although these results are somewhat contradictory to those of Weinraub *et al.* (1984) . . .' (Text 11) [**syntactic reference, with specific citation, intent is to express lack of congruence**]
3. 'In previous conceptual work, including our own, the attention has focused only on . . .' (Text 9) [**syntactic reference, without specific citation, intent is to reassert the gap in the literature**]

In the present corpus, referenced statements appear in *all* moves in the Introductions and Discussion sections except for 'report of findings', evidence that they are employed to support different rhetorical aims.

To examine other problems in identifying the unit of analysis, we can look at a short and accessible extract from one introduction, which instantiates a communicative purpose. The first question that we have to address in identifying a move is 'What is the extent of a move?' The text in Figure 2.1 consists of four units (numbered) that can be defined by communicative intent, but can each unit be considered a separate move?

Various authors have used different criteria for determining the extent of a move. Swales (1990) would recognize unit (1) as a move (**establishing the niche**), (2) as a move (**occupying the niche**) but (3) as Step 2 of the latter move. It is not clear whether he would recognize clause (4) as a separate function. Other authors (Crookes, 1986; possibly Hopkins and Dudley-Evans, 1988) have mapped one move onto one sentence. Thus, clauses 2, 3 and 4 in Figure 2.1 would represent only one move with no further delineation.

There is a diversity of views on determining the extent of a move. Previous literature on Introductions reviewed by Swales and his own study (Swales, 1990) apparently consider moves as larger units, i.e. macro (the next rank after

Figure 2.1   Extract of an Introduction text

---

(1)   N *et al.* note that the exact factors responsible for this apparent salience . . . remain undetermined.

(2)   We report here the results of three studies on one parameter of adult-to-infant speech,

(3)   studies in which we have observed no evidence to support the hypothesis

(4)   that frequency modulation *per se* constitutes a salient feature of the infant's acoustic environment.

From Text 5; see Figure 2.3 for the complete text.

Introductions), than do analysts of Discussions (Belanger, 1982; Dubois, 1997; Hopkins and Dudley-Evans, 1988; McKinlay, 1982; Peng, 1987). In contrast, Gnutzmann and Oldenburg (1991) focus on macro moves in Introductions and Discussions. In no case is the unit of analysis defined. Therefore, no two studies can be compared.

Before we can resolve the question of the extent of the unit of analysis, we need to address two additional basic problems. First, we contend that a rhetorical function is realized in a discourse unit (such as an utterance). That being the case, it does not necessarily co-occur with a grammatical unit such as a sentence because discoursal units can be realized by a variety of grammatical units. To use Berry's example (1981), a morpheme (a unit of meaning) must be distinguished from a syllable (a structural unit). The basic criterion for our units is communicative purpose whether it is mapped onto one clause, several clauses (one complex sentence) (as in sentence 2 of Figure 2.1), or, as we will see later, several sentences (Figure 2.3). (For the sake of brevity, however, we have chosen examples that are composed of only one sentence.) Furthermore, it is important to stress that communicative intent can be expressed in discourse units of different hierarchical ranks (macro and micro units).

To arrive at a uniform yardstick for the extent of the unit of analysis, then, we propose to recognize at least two ranks of units: act and move. The minimal constituent realizing a communicative purpose is an act, while a move is composed of a head act plus slots for pre- and post-head acts. The terminology of Sinclair and Coulthard (1975) captures this hierarchy.[2] The second unit (of meaning) in Figure 2.1 (beginning with sentence 2) can now be seen to be composed of one move which is itself composed of three constituent acts; see Figure 2.2.

Although we have suggested a criterion for identifying units, a second problem is to be able to identify elements from different texts as instantiations of the same communicative purpose. After examining SSR texts, we identified three reoccurring moves, as in Figure 2.3. We did not begin with a set of categories and attempt to match the corpus to the categories.

Moves 1, 2 and 3 express three different purposes and are assigned to

Figure 2.2 Constituents of a move

Previewing the authors' contribution
(2) (HEAD) We report here the results of three studies on one parameter of
adult-to-infant speech,

Reviewing results of the study
(3) (POST-HEAD) studies in which we have observed no evidence to support the
hypothesis

Stating the hypothesis
(4) (POST-HEAD) that frequency modulation *per se* constitutes a salient
feature of the infant's acoustic environment.

---

different categories (later labelled, respectively, **claiming relevance, establishing the gap that present research is to fill**, and **previewing the present authors' contribution**). But how can we account for the variety of realizations of the same move in different texts such as A and B below?

> Move 1:
> A: 'Major changes in work and leisure activities, lifestyles, and mobility patterns have occurred in the US in the last few decades' (Text 2).
> B: 'Over the past decade, many investigators have called for a closer analysis of the language learning environment of the young infant' (Text 5).

Although we discern a shared purpose between A and B, no linguistic feature is common to them and other such instances in the corpus studied.

In order to arrive at an objective definition of each type of unit, we need to set up realization criteria. There are four possible options for systematizing the various realizations of (the head act of) Move 1. First we could look to descriptions in terms of syntactic functions, e.g. 'subject is realized by x', but we soon find that in our corpus this is inadequate, since the subject is not constant in all realizations. In Text 2, for example, the subject is the variables being studied, while in Text 5, the subject is the researchers. A second approach has been to identify moves by lexicogrammatical signals. In analysing service encounters, for instance, Hasan (Halliday and Hasan, 1985) uses lexical signals; if price is discussed, clearly that element can be classified as 'inquiry about price'. Similarly, for Discussion texts, Dudley-Evans (1986, 1994) relies on specific lexical signals. (For example, the lexical items *an examination* or *revealed* are evidence of the report of a finding.) However, in the present study we could not identify any move on the basis of lexical criteria. What we see below, for example, is that the lexeme *finding* is common to (1) an interpretation and (2) a statement of results, therefore negating this as a criterion:

Figure 2.3   Example Introduction text

MOVE 1: CLAIM RELEVANCE

ACT A: **claim relevance for research:**
Over the past decade, many investigators have called for a closer analysis of the language learning environment of the young infant (e.g. N*).

ACT B: **claim relevance for human behaviour:**
Within the recent rapid proliferation of studies of infant audition . . . an area of research has emerged to identify those stimulus parameters that best attract the attention of the young infant and that may contribute to early language learning.

ACT C   **support claim of relevance:**
Previous studies have shown that young infants will selectively attend to novel and familiar auditory stimuli (N* and N*) . . . [*we have deleted the review of literature*]

MOVE 2: ESTABLISH THE GAP THE PRESENT RESEARCH IS MEANT TO FILL

Aslin *et al.* . . . note that the exact factors responsible for this apparent salience . . . remain undetermined.

MOVE 3: PREVIEW THE AUTHORS' CONTRIBUTION

ACT A: **preview**: [*no new paragraph.*] We report here the results of three studies on one parameter of adult-to-infant speech,

ACT B: **review results of the study:**
studies in which we have observed no evidence to support the hypothesis

ACT C: **state the hypothesis:**
that frequency modulation *per se* constitutes a salient feature of the infant's acoustic environment. (Text 5)

N* = name of cited author
Used with the kind permission of the publisher, the Society for Research in Child Development. Analysis has been added.

1. The findings suggest . . .
2. The principal finding is that . . .

Similarly, moves could not be identified by location, i.e. Move 1 was not necessarily the initial move of a text nor did that or any move consistently coincide with the initiation of an orthographic paragraph.

A fourth, more useful approach is suggested by the work of Martin (1985, 1992) in which realizations of each rhetorical function are generated through a system network; this clarifies the kinds of participants and processes necessary in order to realize different acts. Realization rules then specify which of the features from the system network are chosen when other conditions hold.

This approach captures a key aspect which concerns the commonality of the semantic participants in all the realizations in our corpus. As we see in Figure 2.4, each statement contains at least one of the following participants:

a. the research: product or producer (e.g. Text 5 – investigators)
b. the phenomena being studied (e.g. Text 2 – changes)
c. the population affected by the phenomena (e.g. Text 4 – psychotic patients)

The realizations then can be divided into those which claim relevance of the research for human behaviour (Figure 2.4, A) and those which claim relevance for research (Figure 2.4, B).

Secondly, each participant bears some attribute. Selecting the semantic term 'attribute' allows us to include all descriptions, regardless of their grammatical class (e.g. adjective). Some participants bear the attribute **magnitude**, as in

Text 2: **Major** changes in . . .
Text 4: **large numbers** of psychotic patients
Text 5: **many** investigators

So, this addition leads to the following criteria in terms of participants and their attributes:

1. the statement contains participant a, b, or c (above);
2. participant a, b, or c is the bearer of the attribute **magnitude**.

In other realizations another attribute is evident when one of the participants is the bearer of **salience**, e.g. 'The significance of these symptoms is indicated by several surveys in which smokers reported that the onset of withdrawal prompts smoking . . .' (Text 3).

The feature **salience** accounts for the attribute in the realizations in Texts 3, 6, 10, 11 and 12. The final realization in this group is accounted for by addition of the category **intensity**: 'The death of a spouse . . . is one of the **most stressful** events . . .' (Text 8).

With the criteria of semantic components of participants and attributes, we can account for all realizations of Move 1 ('claim relevance'). As we have seen, each example entails that one or more of the participants (the research producers or product, the phenomena, the population) is the bearer of the attribute **magnitude**, salience or intensity forming phrases such as **many investigators, important, most stressful event.** We can then draw a system network which captures the typical choices available in making this realization (Figure 2.5). The system, because of the nature of systems, allows for the expansion of categories if additional features are found, and, in order to complete the analysis, we provide realization rules as in Figure 2.6. This criterion for determining common semantic features and rules for their realization is then applied to each generic structure found. The remaining question is that which concerns the determination of the boundaries of specific elements.

Figure 2.4 Semantic analysis of realizations of 'claim relevance'

Text Number
A. **Relevance is claimed for human behaviour**:

[Phenomenon + Magnitude]

2. **Major** changes in work and leisure activities, lifestyles, and mobility patterns have occurred in the US in the last few decades.

[Population + Magnitude]

4. There is now sufficient evidence that **large numbers of** psychotic patients have an eye-movement dysfunction.

[Phenomenon + Salience]

3. The **significance** of these symptoms is indicated by several surveys in which smokers reported that the onset of withdrawal prompts smoking . . .

6. Early school transitions, such as the transition from preschool to kindergarten, are particularly **important** . . .

10. . . . examining differences between male and female cocaine abusers is potentially clinically **important**.

11. Society suffuses the gender distinction with affect, making gender what is perhaps the **most salient** parameter of social categorization.

12. Resolution of this issue is **important** to understanding the processes that generate emotional feeling.

[Phenomenon + Intensity]

8. The death of a spouse or child is one of the **most stressful** events a person can experience during the course of his or her life.

B. **Relevance is claimed for research**:

[Research Product + Magnitude]

1. Understanding how men and women react to circumstances they consider to be unfair has been the focus of a **growing** literature.

[Research Producers + Magnitude]

5. Over the past decade, **many** investigators have called for a closer analysis of the language learning environment of the young infant.

7. The alleged biases of television newscasters have been a topic of discussion for **many** years.

9. . . . the study of effects of social conditions on the diffusion of distress and disease in the population **can be traced to** . . . 1897.

Underlining = participant; bold = claim

Figure 2.5 A partial system network for features of the head act of Move 1, 'claim relevance'

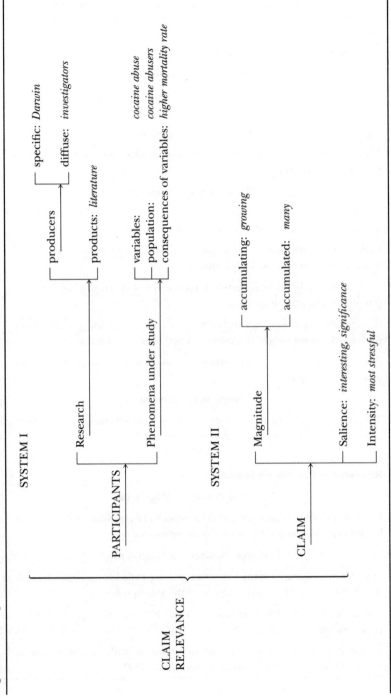

The items in italics are examples of realizations.

Figure 2.6 Realization rules for the head act of Move 1, 'claim relevance'

Variation A: Claim relevance for research

FEATURE	REALIZATION
Participants	
Phenomena under study	Aim of research
Research	
producers	*investigators*
products	*analysis, focus, study, topic*
Claim	
Magnitude	attribute of [Research: producers or products]: *growing* literature; topic of discussion for *many years*

Example: 'Over the past decade, many investigators [MAGNITUDE + PRODUCER] have called for a closer analysis of the language learning environment of the young infant . . . [AIM OF RESEARCH] (Text 5).

Variation B: Claim relevance for human behaviour

FEATURE	REALIZATION
Participants	
Phenomena under study	Affector
Population	Affected: *psychotic patients*
Claim	
Magnitude	*large numbers*
Intensity	*most stressful*
Salience	*importance* = Attribute of Affected, Affector, or Consequences of Affector

Examples: 'There is now sufficient evidence that large numbers of psychotic patients [MAGNITUDE + AFFECTED] have an eye-movement dysfunction [AFFECTOR]' (Text 4).

  'The death of a spouse . . . is one of the most stressful events [AFFECTOR + INTENSITY] that a person can experience' (Text 8).

  'These potential differences assume particular importance in the light of the higher mortality of women alcoholics when compared with their male counterparts . . . [SALIENCE + CONSEQUENCES OF AFFECTOR]' (Text 10).

In some genres, such as school lessons, there are customary boundary markers between moves. However, the texts in our corpus revealed no universal lexico-grammatical or formal markers to indicate the initiation of a move. The boundaries of an act or a move do not co-occur with boundaries of grammatical elements such as sentences or paragraphs, as we see in the text in Figure 2.3, Move 3. The minimal unit in which an act can be realized is a finite clause, but theoretically there is no upper limit. On the other hand, a complex sentence can realize more than one rhetorical function, as we indicated in Figure 2.1, sentence 2. Furthermore, moves are not always presented in linear order (Move 1–2–3), so they cannot be identified by location.

In spite of the lack of boundary markers, moves can generally be differentiated from one another because, as we have specified, a move consists of an obligatory [head] act plus slots for optional acts. When the head [obligatory] act is the initial act in the move, the boundary is clear, i.e. the move begins with the act which carries the realization features for that move. Thus, Move 2 realizes a topic shift from the positive to the 'negative' features of past research (sometimes marked by a signal of counter expectation such as *although*, *while* and *however*). Move 3 invariably changes the topic to the product or producers of current research, e.g. 'In this paper, we present . . .'. (The realization rules for these moves are presented in Chapter 3.) The text in Figure 2.3 reflects the ideal state in that head acts are initial acts and Moves 1–2–3 are presented linearly.

However, when the head act is not the initial act, or when the move sequence is not linear, a decision must be made as to whether a certain text segment represents a post-head of the preceding move or a pre-head of the subsequent move. In general, we made such decisions on internal evidence – logical relations, either marked by connectors or inferred (as in Figure 2.7). The broad categories of logical relations which can connect contiguous acts to a head act to form a move are outlined below. These categories originate in the work of Halliday and Hasan (1976), Halliday (1985), and Ventola (1987) but have been expanded to accommodate our data.

   a. continuity – where an act enlarges, clarifies, reinforces or reformulates [the claim in] an adjacent act. This relationship is sometimes signalled lexically (e.g. **furthermore**, **in fact**, **similarly**). This category includes metacomments that introduce a move, e.g. 'There are several possible explanations for [x]';

   b. reasoning – where an act is a premise or conclusion in inductive or deductive reasoning. This relationship is sometimes signalled lexically (**in conclusion**, **therefore**, **if . . . then**);

   c. support – where an act specifies, exemplifies, justifies or presents evidence for [a claim in] an adjacent act. This relationship is sometimes signalled lexically (**for example**, **specifically**);

   d. comment – where an act expresses the author's opinion about an adjacent act (e.g. '. . . **the interesting and disturbing element of this research is the possibility that . . .**' Text 7).

Figure 2.7 Example of the structure of a move: offering interpretation*

Pre-head: authors announce that interpretation will follow

(1) 'In contrast with patients with affective disorders, the coupling of eye-movement dysfunction and thought disorder in schizophrenic patients can be explained differently.'

Pre-head: authors report what is known about the general phenomenon under study

[CONTINUITY]

(2) 'The central nervous system disorder suggested by eye-tracking impairments . . . represents a hypothesized latent trait.'

Head: authors offer hypothesis

[REASONING]

(3) 'The results of the present study suggest that thought disorder in schizophrenics may be another manifestation of this latent trait.'

Post-head: authors claim support for hypothesis

[SUPPORT]

(4) 'This formulation is supported by the evidence that . . .'

(Text 4)
*Logical connectors are in square brackets.

These account for all of the logical relations that figure significantly in our data and that determine the status of the pre- or post-head of a move.

Summary

In this book, we focus on the analysis of research texts (first-hand reports of hypothesis-testing research). Because genre analysis of such texts has not yet developed a consistent methodology, we propose a method that we hope will allow for the comparison of texts in different academic fields; this comparison should ultimately be of value to novice writers in different fields, and analysts of other genres.

Our model for genre analysis provides several new criteria:

1. Generic structures are defined in terms of rhetorical functions which convey communicative intent, e.g. offering a hypothesis. This leads to two results. First, discourse units are disengaged from grammatical units such as the clause or sentence. Second, 'References to previous literature' are

not considered moves *per se*, but are classified according to their communicative intent.

2. Realizations for each generic structure are provided in terms of classes of semantic attributes, rather than specific lexicogrammatical signals.

3. The units of analysis are distinguished by rank, i.e. the minimal unit expressing a rhetorical function is an **act**, and the next higher rank of function is a **move** (Sinclair and Coulthard, 1975). A move is composed of one obligatory act (the head) and slots for optional acts (pre-head and post-head).

4. The criterion for inclusion of optional acts within a move is the logical relation of the optional act to the head act.

5. We consider moves that characterize a genre as **prototypical** rather than **obligatory**; as we will show in Chapter 4, all structures do not have to be present to realize an instance of the genre.

Notes

1. '*Ex post facto* research is systematic empirical inquiry in which the scientist does not have direct control of independent variables because their manifestations have already occurred or because they are inherently not manipulable. Inferences about relations among variables are made, without direct intervention from concomitant variation of independent and dependent variables' (Kerlinger, 1973: 379).

2. The remainder of Sinclair and Coulthard's terminology and method is particular to the genre they studied; we are only using their terminology for determining the ranks of discourse elements.

3 Setting the stage: analysis of Introduction sections

Introduction

In Chapter 1, we explained that characterizing expository text by genre first of all means determining the customary discourse structures (moves and their constituent acts); these in turn are defined by their communicative purposes. The notion of 'genre' presupposes a set of socially prescribed events; we say a text belongs to a genre because it encapsulates most of the structures we have come to expect from that genre. This seems, at first glance, to be a rather mechanical interpretation and one which would constrain any would-be writer. It can be argued, however, that genre structure is analogous to iambic pentameter and stanzas in poetry; against these 'constraints' an infinite number of poems can be written. In fact, if the genre imposes a prescribed order on texts, why are texts rhetorically so different from one another (in addition to their differences in ideational content)? Why do some seem provocative or threatening while others are more sensitive to the feelings of the reader?

In this chapter, we show the genre structures and then explain some of the options available within each structure for the authors to further their rhetorical aims. We refer to the rhetorical aims as the 'interpersonal' aspects of each move in keeping with Halliday's (1973: 58) meaning of the term, i.e. the interpersonal metafunction is concerned with:

> language as a mediator of role, including all that can be understood by the expression of our own personality and personal feelings on the one hand, and the forms of interaction and social interplay with other participants in the communication situation on the other hand.

We have extended *interpersonal* to refer to that stratum of meaning intended to affect the reader. In the words of Weimar (1977: 14): 'Whenever a scientist communicates even the most mundane and seemingly innocuous descriptions, he is persuading his audience, literally commanding them, to adopt his point of view'.

To carry the argument further, distinguishing between genre structures and interpersonal/rhetorical is somewhat arbitrary. After all, if we consider not genre, which is a construct of the social world, but the 'facts' of the physical/natural world, the essential parts of a research text are the report of the author's findings and a description of his/her methods in order to allow for replication. Indeed, as we pointed out in Chapter 1, these are the core of the earliest texts in English, as the following 'introduction' communicated to the Royal Society in 1717 attests. Here, the author carefully dissociates himself from making any interpretation:

> According to these laudable Examples [of Hippocrates, Galen and other Fathers of Medicine] I shall, for the Satisfaction of the Curious and Ingenious, give a true and faithful Account of an extraordinary Excrescence cut off from the cheek of a Man. . . . I have given a true and plain Account of this extraordinary Case from certain Information; I have contented myself to relate only Matters of Fact, without making any Observations or Reflections on it; for I leave it to the Philosophers and Virtuosi to make their own Reasonings and Refinements as seems best to themselves. (Valle, 1997: 86)

However, today such a report of bare 'facts' does not suffice; it must be prefaced by an introduction, carefully motivating the research, and a discussion, validating, justifying and sometimes extolling the findings. In contemporary Introductions to social science research texts, at least, the authors fulfil three major purposes. Although in our corpus these moves were always present, authors may choose to omit one, given certain constraints. This in itself is a rhetorical choice; while the types of moves are 'given', the option of omitting one is available.

The key moves

In Move 1, *claim relevance of field*, the authors justify their choice of phenomena for intensive study by appealing to its significance, importance or worthwhileness.[1] In ideational terms, they define the parameters of the academic field that they are studying. In Move 2, the authors seek some no-man's-land upon which to set up stakes; we have labelled this *establish the gap the present research is meant to fill*, in which the authors point out that the knowledge about the phenomena that they have chosen is incomplete.[2] Lastly, the authors declare that they have taken possession. In Move 3, *preview the authors' contribution*, they declare that they have carried out an investigation into the specific field. In this genre, the declaration entails the promise that the detailed account of this investigation represents the content of the article to follow.

In order to highlight these moves, we contrast the head act of these moves, as given in Figure 2.3, with the first paragraph of a polemic article in science. (There is no labelled Introduction in this text but the first paragraph can be read as such since it is a blueprint statement of the contents of the article.)

Research text:
Move 1 – 'Over the past decade, many investigators have called for a closer analysis of the language learning environment of the young infant [references are given].'

Move 2 – '[N] *et al.* note that the exact factors responsible for this apparent salience . . . remain undetermined.'
Move 3 – 'We report here the results of three studies . . .'

Polemic text:

The use of animals for research and testing is only one of many investigative techniques available. We believe that although animal experiments are sometimes intellectually seductive, they are poorly suited to addressing the urgent health problems of our era, such as . . . Even worse, animal experiments can mislead researchers . . . by failing to predict the toxic effects of drugs. Fortunately, other, more reliable methods that represent a far better investment of research funds can be employed (Barnard and Kaufman, 1997: 64).

To recall, a move can be realized by only the head act, e.g. Move 2 – '[N] *et al.* note that the exact factors responsible for this apparent salience . . . remain undetermined' or it can incorporate many other acts to strengthen or explain the head act as depicted in Figure 2.3. The result is that the components of instantial moves can differ from one another. Table 3.1 illustrates possible component acts of the moves in Introductions.

How are moves realized in texts?

Our method for objectively defining Moves 1, 2 and is demonstrated in Chapter 2. To recall, these moves are defined in terms of an open set of semantic features for *relevance, gap* and *preview* rather than specific lexicogrammatical structures. Why this is necessary is evidenced by the variety of ways that relevance can be asserted, for example, '[x problem] has been the focus of a growing literature' (Text 1), or 'Major changes in work and leisure activities . . . have occurred' (Text 2). To capture the common semantic features in such diverse realizations, we provide a set of options for each move, as in Figure 2.5. Thus, the criteria for claiming relevance can be expressed in selections from the systems shown. The categories can be expanded if new types of realizations are found in additional texts. The system network and realization rules for Move 1 have been presented in Chapter 2, as Figures 2.5 and 2.6, respectively. The system networks and realization rules for Move 2 are presented in Figures 3.1, 3.2 and 3.3. The system network and realization rules for Move 3 are presented in Figures 3.4 and 3.5, respectively. These will be discussed in turn.

Embedding the author's aims in the key moves

Faced with the predetermined structures of the genre, the author can nevertheless decide how to realize them or even ignore them for certain reasons. The interpersonal level represents a more delicate scale of options within each move and leaves room for manipulating one's rhetorical aims.

Table 3.1 Component acts of 'moves' in Introduction sections of research texts

---

MOVE 1 – CLAIMING RELEVANCE OF FIELD

Obligatory:

a. Asserting relevance of field of which research is a part

b. Reporting what is known about phenomena under study, e.g.:
'Throughout childhood, children participate in a variety of ecological transitions that require adaptation to new or altered environments (Bronfenbrenner, 1979)' (Text 2).

Optional:

a. Making assertions about the research process of others, e.g.:
'Much of the empirical work on distributive justice over the past two decades has been done within an experimental paradigm' (Text 1).

b. Reporting terminology conventions, e.g.:
'Rationalization bias refers to the possibility that . . .' (Text 3).

c. Reporting conclusions drawn by previous authors, e.g.:
'Cohen and Felson (1979) argue that the dispersion of activity away from the household and new manufacturing technologies . . . correspond to temporal changes in rates of criminal victimization' (Text 2).

d. Drawing [own] conclusions about the research of others, e.g.:
'Given what we now know about the child's active construction of categories during the first 2 years, the original idea that parents' reaction and children's sex typing should be directly related seems naive' (Text 11).

e. Metacomments, e.g.:
'[However, since both theories presume that . . .], they are treated here as complementary approaches' (Text 2).

f. Narrowing parameters of field, e.g.:
'In the present investigation, a particularly subtle mode of influence is considered . . .' (Text 7).

MOVE 2 – ESTABLISHING THE GAP PRESENT RESEARCH IS MEANT TO FILL

Obligatory:

Pointing out deficiencies in the present state of knowledge

Optional:

a. Positing an ideal way to fill the gap that has just been created, e.g.:
'Systematic prospective studies . . . would prevent both the problems of self retrospective designs' (Text 3).

b. Mitigating – Pointing out positive contribution of previous research, e.g.:
'While this research has advanced a number of useful generalizations . . .' (Text 1).

c. Reporting what is known about phenomena under study

Table 3.1   (*continued*)

MOVE 3 – PREVIEWING AUTHORS' NEW ACCOMPLISHMENTS

Obligatory:

Stating purpose of present study or contents of article

Optional:

a. **Positing an ideal way to fill the gap that has just been created** (Move 2, **a.** above)

b. **Reporting what is known about phenomena under study**

c. **Justifying hypotheses**, e.g.:
'This hypothesis [above] is based on the premise that the range of peers . . .' (Text 6).

d. **Disclosing whether hypotheses have been confirmed or not**, e.g.:
'The results of the study do not confirm the hypothesis that tobacco withdrawal reduces success at smoking cessation' (Text 3).

e. **Summarizing methods**, e.g.:
'For this reason, each . . . respondent in the present investigation was matched with a control respondent' (Text 8).

f. **Presenting hypotheses or research questions**, e.g.:
'It is also possible that the degree to which children are liked by classmates . . . depends upon the range of peers with whom they interact' (Text 6).

Move 1: 'claim relevance for present research'

Apparently, a statement such as 'The purpose of this study is to . . .' is necessary but not sufficient as an Introduction. The authors must justify their choice of phenomena for intensive study but can choose from a range of positive qualities such as *significance, importance* or *worthwhileness*. In all our texts, no really new information is given in Move 1 but we have chosen a particularly dramatic example from outside the corpus to highlight this fact. Rather than preview with the economical 'The following is a study of divorce in the US . . .', the authors make an assertion so obvious that it seems superfluous: 'Marital dissolution is a serious social issue in terms of its negative consequences for the mental and physical health of spouses . . . and their children [References are given]' (Text 13).

Furthermore, although lexical choices from each of two systems are sufficient to realize 'relevance', e.g. X phenomenon [system I] is of major [system II] significance (see Figure 2.5), authors can make this relevance more persuasive by (1) specifying, depending upon their audience, whether the relevance is directed to research or to human behaviour; (2) widening the relevance by directing it to a more general, rather than a specific phenomenon, and (3) locating the relevance in a more extensive and/or recent time frame. We now discuss these in greater detail.

Deciding for whom or what to claim relevance

In this corpus, the claims of relevance go beyond a mere declaration that *[X] is an interesting/important topic* to orienting this relevance toward one of two value systems: research (a, below) or human behaviour (b, below):

  a. 'Over the past decade, many investigators have called for a closer analysis of the language learning environment of the young infant [References]' (Text 5).
  b. 'These potential differences assume particular importance in light of the higher mortality of women alcoholics when compared with their male counterparts' (Text 10).

This choice probably is dependent upon the perspective of the journal as either theoretical or applied. Studies in research-oriented moves are justified by the claim that they are part of a major trend, which seems to involve a tautology – this research is relevant because there is so much research:

  a. 'Over the past decade, many investigators have called for . . .' (Text 5).
  b. 'The process governing the distribution of rewards in society has been a central concern for sociologists of diverse theoretical orientations (References)' (Text 1).

The choice of 'research' orientation can nevertheless evoke the recognition of social conscience on the part of the author, as in 'The alleged biases of television newscasters have been a topic of discussion for many years . . . the interesting and disturbing element of this research is the possibility that the biased news might affect those who watch it' (Text 7).

Expanding or contracting the area of relevance

Claiming relevance includes a further interpersonal option, which is mapped onto a particular phenomenon (ideational element). Thus, relevance can be claimed for a broader field than the narrow one that was actually studied. For instance, in Text 7, the general field of (a) *The alleged biases of television newscasters* is eventually narrowed to (b) *the effect of the newscasters' facial expressions on the voting behaviour of those who view the news.*

A statement of the specific parameters as in (b), above, is obligatory; these are the variables that will be dealt with in the study and are usually stated in the title. If the general field (a) is realized also, then Move 1 (relevance) is claimed for the general field. Most authors prefer to establish relevance for the general field, rather than for the specific parameters, even though this requires additional work.

In addition to being non-efficient, mapping relevance onto the general field seems non-functional, since we are told that scientists do not read papers sequentially but employ various schemata for quickly focusing on the 'new' information (Bazerman, 1985; Bruce, personal communication; and Huckin, 1987, cited in Swales, 1990). If so, the intended reader will quickly skip the 'general field'. Since the majority of authors extend relevance to the most general field possible, it must have a rhetorical function, namely, strengthening the claim.

It is also possible to reiterate relevance, mapping it onto increasingly specific fields, as in the following passage. The relevance feature is italicized.

> [General field]: *Throughout childhood*, children participate in **a variety of ecological transitions** that require adaptation. [Specific field: first level]: Past research suggests that the interpersonal demands and corresponding outcomes of **school transitions** are *also important* in forecasting later social and school adjustment. [Specific field: second level]: Early school transitions, such as **the transition from preschool to kindergarten**, are *particularly important*. (Text 6)

Delineating the time frame of relevance: timelessness or recency

In addition to choosing the appropriate value (research or behaviour) and a broader intellectual field on which to map relevance, another sign of interpersonal considerations here is that authors convey relevance by bringing the time frame close to the reader. All Move 1 head acts (relevance) are, by definition, in current time (realized by the present simple or present perfect tense of the verbs). One text uses the present progressive, a rare choice, suggesting that authors may violate the stylistic norm to express 'recency': 'Theories of this general sort are gaining increasing acceptance . . .' (Text 12).

Not all claims of relevance can be situated in recent time. If the orientation is towards research, it is relatively easy to situate the research process within a recent time frame. However, an orientation towards human behaviour usually entails timelessness, and thus conflicts with recency. The conflict faced by researchers, then, is between the 'people' value or the 'time' value. The conflict is resolved by situating human behaviour phenomena in recent time, as in 'Major changes in work and leisure activities . . . have occurred in the US in the last few decades' (Text 2). Recency can be reasserted in support of this move (the literature review), as in 'We have recently presented results . . .' (Text 9).

Move 2: 'establish the gap the present research is meant to fill'

All three moves allow for input of varying degrees by the author. However, it is worth discussing Move 2, 'establish the gap', at greater length since it seems to be the generic structure in the Introduction that is potentially the most interpersonal of the three moves. A claim of relevance need only state that *[x phenomenon] is important for study because* . . . What is important is admittedly relative but we can allow for a universe in which every phenomenon is worthy of study. Move 3 need only announce the purpose of the present research; surely an incontrovertible fact which the author has the right to assert. Both of these moves do not tread on the toes of other citizens of the academic universe. However, establishing the gap can lead to direct confrontation, as shown in the following excerpt by a novice engineering student: 'Jones (1992) and Smith

(1993) built experimental systems which utilise the FM–SW technique. Their reports did not suggest any solution to the mutual interference problem. Although Jones claimed to have one, they have not published it.'

The first observation is that Moves 1 and 3 could be sufficient for an Introduction. Move 2 is not universal among biology reports, for example (L. Lewin, L. Ayalon, personal communications). It can be artificially created as the following text in our corpus illustrates (emphasis and names of moves added):

> [Move 1, RELEVANCE] – There is now sufficient evidence that large numbers of psychotic patients have an eye-movement dysfunction [followed by a literature review]. *An early study* of eye-tracking dysfunction in schizophrenia reported a relationship between thought disorder and smooth-pursuit impairments ... The relationship between thought disorder and eye-tracking dysfunctions, while not high, was statistically significant. [Move 2, GAP] – *Since that time, there have been no further reports on the association between thought disorder and eye-movement abnormalities.* [Move 3, PREVIEW] – We present a replication of the finding of an association between thought disorder and eye-tracking dysfunctions. (Text 4)

The 'early study' referred to was done in 1974, while Text 4 was published in January 1987. 'Since that time . . .' is a unique type of realization for the gap. If the authors intend to suggest that eye movement dysfunctions might have changed in 12 years, this sentence is illogical. It is also unnecessary, since the next sentence affirms that the present study is a replication. (Compare the acceptability of the following created text: 'The relationship between thought disorder and eye-tracking dysfunctions, while not high, was statistically significant. We present a replication of the study.') The creation of a gap-statement, when no gap seems evident, suggests that a slot exists in the genre for this move, even if its realization provides no new information.

Deciding whether to hedge or to fence: gaps of defect, scarcity and obscurity

The first rhetorical step, then, is to realize this move of establishing a gap. The second is to decide how much prominence to afford it. To recall, communicative purposes are realized in moves, which, in turn, are composed of one or more acts (each realizing a subpurpose). Therefore, the minimal realization is one act, as in 'Aslin *et al.* note that the exact factors responsible for this apparent salience . . . remain undetermined'. However, a text can realize more than one instance of 'establishing the gap'. In the following example, Move 2 encompasses at least three acts that establish the gap: 'The major problems with previous tests of the theories involve . . .; . . . such measures fail to consider . . .; . . . most tests of the theories have examined only . . .' (Text 2). The present subcorpus was composed of all acts which realize 'establish the gap', totalling 45 acts from the twelve texts.

The next most delicate option is the **type of claim** that will realize the gap. The following examples indicate a variety of claims which share a common communicative purpose:

1. 'Many previous studies on [x] have not included control or comparison groups . . .' (Text 8).

Figure 3.1 A partial system network for features of the head act of Move 2, 'establish the gap'

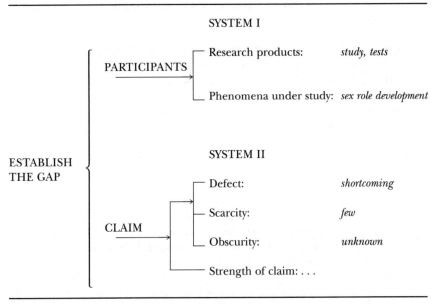

SYSTEM I

PARTICIPANTS
— Research products: *study, tests*
— Phenomena under study: *sex role development*

ESTABLISH THE GAP

SYSTEM II

CLAIM
— Defect: *shortcoming*
— Scarcity: *few*
— Obscurity: *unknown*
— Strength of claim: . . .

The items in italics are examples of realizations.

2. 'Since that time, there have been no further reports . . .' (Text 4).
3. '. . . the impact of such losses . . . remains largely unexamined' (Text 8).

Even within the first type of claim, we can perceive a common communicative purpose but no common lexicogrammatical feature in the realizations, as in the following examples:

a. '. . . previous applications of these theories are limited in several respects' (Text 2).
b. 'The major problems with previous tests of the theories involve . . .' (Text 2).
c. 'Many previous studies on [x] have not included control or comparison groups in the design . . .' (Text 8).

We therefore distinguish between the different types of claims on the basis of semantic criteria. Semantic features for 'establish the gap' are selected from the systems in Figure 3.1.

Establishing realization rules in terms of semantic features from paradigmatic networks (e.g. Figure 3.1) allows us to classify an adjective (*limited*) and a nominal group (*The major problems*) as attributes of the research product (*theories, tests*). It also allows us to include acts such as (c) above, which, on a superficial reading, are of the agent (*Many previous studies*) / process (*have not included*) type, as essentially describing a defect in the research. Further details of the realization rules are given in Figure 3.2.

The primary options in the claim networks are defined and exemplified as follows (features are in square brackets):

[**defect**]: research exists and is found defective, e.g. 'Many previous studies on [x] have not included control or comparison groups . . .' (Text 8);

[**scarcity**]: research does not exist or is scarce, e.g. 'Since that time, there have been no further reports . . .' (Text 4);

[**obscurity**]: X factor is obscure, e.g. 'The impact of such losses . . . remains largely unexamined' (Text 8).

With the choice of [obscurity] the authors need not commit themselves as to whether previous research exists or whether existing research is defective. Authors can choose one, two, or all three types of claims in realizing Move 2.

The generic structure of research articles allows the author to express his/her perspective within each move including 'establishing the gap'. To summarize, authors can choose among claims of *defect*, *scarcity* or *obscurity* in establishing the gap. In the last two options, the authors skirt around the necessity of criticizing existing research, since the research product can be omitted ('The impact of such losses . . . remains largely unexamined' Text 8) or its existence can be negated ('Since that time, there have been no further reports . . .' Text 4). In contrast, in selecting [claim: defect], authors throw down the gauntlet and perhaps invite counter accusations ('Although a number of descriptive studies of cocaine abusers have been published [references], these reports have not differentiated between the sexes' Text 10). The most neutral choice would seem to be *scarcity* as in 'There is very little research on the role of women in drug abuse' [created text].

We have presented what we term 'options'. One might counter that the type of claim an author makes (*scarcity*, *obscurity* or *defect*) is not optional but con-strained by 'reality'. Surely, a claim of 'previous literature is scarce' is an objective fact. Since it is difficult to verify the scarcity of data in unfamiliar fields, we report a claim of scarcity from a field with which we are familiar: 'However, with few exceptions (e.g. Higgins, 1981; Premo and Stiles, 1983), little attention has been paid to the role of language use in social interaction' (Holtgraves, 1986). This quotation is from one of the journals in the corpus but not one of the twelve texts in the sample. The author's claim that 'little empirical attention has been paid' would surely be contested by applied linguists and sociolinguists among us.

Similarly, one might expect that choice of claim is dependent upon whether or not the author has cited literature; specifically, a claim of defect 'Many previous studies on [x] have not included control or comparison groups . . .' (Text 8) must co-occur with a referent (i.e. a citation of previous research), while a claim of scarcity/obscurity has no referent.

However, even when specific research has been cited, authors can opt for *scarcity* or *obscurity* as in 1 and 2 below, which follow a review of previous studies:

Figure 3.2 Realization rules for features of the head act of Move 2, 'establish the gap'

Variation A: Claim that existing research is defective	
FEATURE	REALIZATION
Participants:	
Research products	Bearer, realized by nominal group representing research: *tests, reports*
Claim:	
Defect	Attribute of Bearer, realized by: nominal group: *problem, concern* adjective: *limited, inaccurate* verbal group:
	1. negative value verb: *fail, lack*
	2. negative value verbal group: positive value verb: *test* AND negation: *not*

Variation B: Claim that existing research is scarce	
FEATURE	REALIZATION
Research products	Bearer: *tests, reports*
Claim:	
Scarcity	Attribute of Bearer, realized by: determiner
	1. minimizer: *few, only*
	2. negator: *no*
	adjective: *rare*

Variation C: Claim that X factor is obscure	
FEATURE	REALIZATION
Phenomenon under study	Bearer: a research variable
Claim:	
Obscurity	Attribute of Bearer, realized by: lack of research process: *unexamined* lack of cognizance: *little is known*

1. 'Aslin *et al.* note that the exact factors responsible for this apparent salience ... remain undetermined' (Text 5).
2. 'No theory gives us a coherent account of the total process of sex-role development' (Text 11).

The choice between *scarcity, obscurity* or *defect* may be constrained by the reality of the research field; however, the author has considerable latitude in determining how to present the claim. The reader then must interpret the choice of *scarcity, obscurity* or *defect* against the background of the reality of the research field and as a rejection of the two options that were not chosen.

Strengthening or diluting the claim

After choosing the type of claim, above, authors can manipulate the strength of this claim. In some types of manipulations, known as *hedging*, writers modify their responsibility for the truth-value of an utterance or even hide their attitude (Markkanen and Schröder, 1987). One might assume that scientists will hedge because 'hedges are part of a wider system of politeness designed to redress the threat research claims contain to the "face" of other scientists' (Myers, 1985, 1989, cited in Hyland, 1996: 434). On the other hand, one could expect that scientists, commonly regarded as impersonal and very economical in language, will be impervious to social nuances. Interestingly, we find a range from 'maximum strength' statements such as 'No theory gives us a coherent account of the total process of sex-role development' (Text 11) to 'diluted strength' statements such as 'As a number of investigators have noted, a major aspect of grief about which little is known is its duration . . .' (Text 8). This variation in the strength of claim is formalized in the two systems in Figure 3.3.

Authors can temper the strength of their claim by distancing themselves from the degree of responsibility that will be encoded (System 1, ASSIGNMENT OF RESPONSIBILITY, Figure 3.3). (We assume that, in practice, the author identifies with any unattributed statement of 'gap' that he/she does not refute. We refer now only to the semantic realization of distance.) Authors can accept total responsibility (no perceiver is realized), e.g. 'No theory gives us a coherent account . . .' (Text 11), or dilute responsibility by expressing the gap as a product of human perception. Within this latter category, authors can locate the perception within their own cognition, i.e. by selecting [non-omniscient], or within the cognition of outsiders.

At the other extreme, they can evade responsibility by projecting the perception of a gap entirely onto an outsider, as in 'Aslin *et al.* note that the exact factors responsible for this apparent salience . . . remain undetermined' (Text 5). Between these two extremes (total or no responsibility), the alternative of partial responsibility may be expressed. The responsibility may be mitigated if the feature [non-omniscient] is chosen by acknowledging human limitations, as in 'To our knowledge, no studies have examined the physical impact . . .' (Text 8). When [Outsiders] is chosen, a still more delicate option can be exercised by explicitly including oneself within the attribution, e.g. 'As a number

Figure 3.3 A partial system network for features of 'strength of the claim'

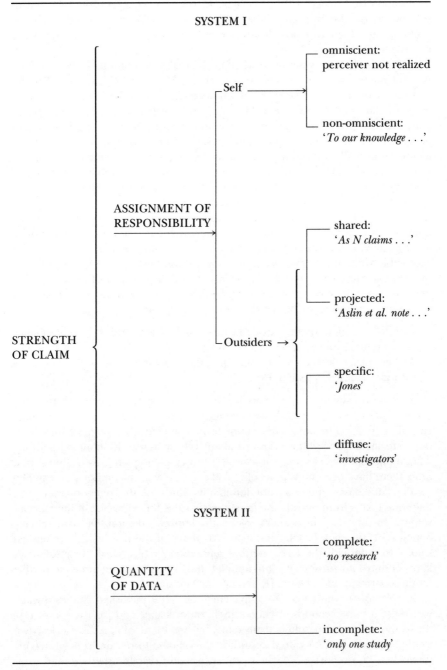

SYSTEM I

SYSTEM II

STRENGTH
OF CLAIM

ASSIGNMENT OF
RESPONSIBILITY

Self

omniscient:
perceiver not realized

non-omniscient:
'*To our knowledge . . .*'

Outsiders →

shared:
'*As N claims . . .*'

projected:
'*Aslin et al. note . . .*'

specific:
'*Jones*'

diffuse:
'*investigators*'

QUANTITY
OF DATA

complete:
'*no research*'

incomplete:
'*only one study*'

Items in italics are examples of realizations.

of investigators have noted, a major aspect of grief about which little is known is its duration (Reference, 1981)' (Text 8). In yet another option the selection of [Outsiders] can be [specific], in which case the perceiver is named (*Aslin*), or [diffuse], in which case a collective term, such as *a number of investigators*, is realized as perceiver.

The question now arises as to whether the realization of a perceiver [Self] or [Outsiders] weakens or strengthens the claim. Myers (1989) assumes that the realization of the first person pronoun weakens claims. In Hyland's view of scientific claims in general (1996: 447), 'an overt acceptance of personal responsibility mitigates the expression of a proposition and signifies a reader-oriented hedge'. Paradoxically, acceptance of responsibility strengthens the author's identification with the claim yet weakens the claim itself. In linguistic terms, it reduces factivity. The question of whether assigning responsibility to outsiders [shared] or [projected] strengthens or weakens the claim is even more complicated. In theory, a categorical assertion ('No theory gives us a coherent account . . .' [Text 11]) is a fact of the material world, not a judgement of the human mind. In the practice of scientific research texts, however, attribution is a major device for strengthening claims; in fact, no research text would be acceptable without reference to previous literature. Sentence (1) below indicates that the gap has been perceived by at least one other perceiver (*Aslin et al.*), while in (2) the author may be alone in his/her perception. It remains a matter of conjecture whether (1) or (2) below is the stronger claim:

1. Aslin *et al.* note that the exact factors responsible for this apparent salience . . . remain undetermined' (Text 5).
2. The exact factors responsible for this apparent salience . . . remain undetermined' (created text).

The second system which offers features for strengthening or weakening the claim is QUANTITY OF DATA. When choosing claims of *scarcity* or *obscurity*, authors can place this claim on a continuum from complete ('no research has been done') to incomplete ('little is known about [x]' or 'research about [x] is rare'). The implication of selecting [QUANTITY OF DATA: complete], as in 'Since that time, there have been no reports of . . .' (Text 4), is that the author has searched all the data bases, and has not found one study of the phenomenon. The following text is from outside the immediate corpus but from one of the journals studied. In this case, the authors answer the implicit question 'Did you actually search ALL the data bases?' and assure us that 'Of the nearly 1200 published studies to date with the terms marital separation or divorce in their titles, we know of only four prospective longitudinal studies that have attempted to predict future separation and divorce [References]' (Text 13).

In spite of the undeniable completeness of '1200 published studies' (which would seem to be grounds to choose [Self: omnisicient] and [DATA: complete]), the authors choose to soften their stand by 'we know of . . .'. These last two examples again demonstrate that authors can choose to refrain from protecting themselves ('no reports . . .') when prudence might dictate otherwise and, conversely, may choose to exercise caution even though their case is strong.

These two systems (ASSIGNMENT OF RESPONSIBILITY and QUANTITY OF DATA) seem to be independent. That is, authors can use neither, one, or both kinds of hedges. A choice of [QUANTITY OF DATA: complete] can co-occur with partial acceptance of responsibility [Self: non-omniscient], as in 'To our knowledge, no studies have examined the psychological impact . . .' (Text 8). Conversely, total acceptance of responsibility can co-occur with [QUANTITY OF DATA: incomplete], as in 'Indeed, the drug abuse literature in general has paid relatively little attention to women' (Text 10). Other combinations of features can be generated from the two systems in Figure 3.3.

The next important issue concerns the relationship between the two levels of delicacy: type of claim and acceptance of responsibility. In claims of *defect*, authors usually accept total responsibility. That is, the perceiver of the specific defect is the author [Self] alone. However, in a minority of cases authors choose to hide behind an outsider, as in 'Winton (1986) has recently observed that the nature of this . . . effect is unclear because the number of expression conditions used in the research is usually too small' (Text 12). As opposed to claims of *defect*, claims of *scarcity* and *obscurity* are about equally divided between those for which the authors accept partial responsibility and those for which they accept total responsibility. Furthermore, only claims of *scarcity* or *obscurity* select the feature [non-omniscient] so we find, for example, 'To our knowledge, no studies have examined the psychological impact . . .' (Text 8) but not 'To our knowledge, previous research has failed to include control groups' [created text].

Although genres are defined by structures that realize communicative purposes, once the basic options that define the genre are chosen, authors can choose from a range of options to construct interpersonal relations. For instance, authors can select features to 'establish the gap' that will avoid head-on criticisms of specific researchers, or they can choose to make a claim that previous research is defective. They can avoid mentioning previous research by claiming that knowledge about the phenomenon under study is scarce or obscure. If they choose [Defect], they can mitigate the claim by making the bearer of the defect a class ('Much previous research has not . . .') instead of an individual. The harshness of a claim of defect can also be mitigated by a preceding clause stressing the accomplishments of previous research, as in 'While this research has advanced a number of useful generalisations . . . , one of its major shortcomings has been its failure to . . .' (Text 1). In still another approach, the authors pay a compliment in the general introduction ('In a path-breaking set of papers, this group [Jasso–Alves–Rossi] has taken up the task of quantifying . . .' (Text 1), but deal a blow in the subsequent detailed review of the literature (['Jasso–Alves–Rossi] have overlooked the critical role of . . .' Text 1).

We have presented above some options for reducing risk and avoiding collision with one's colleagues. But these options are not universally exercised. Lest we are left with the impression that social scientists are excessively polite, note the following excerpt from outside the immediate corpus but from one of the journals studied: 'The problem is not in the logic. The problem is the data – more precisely the lack of data. The data Wilson presents does [sic] not address the issue of mobility at all' (Text 14). Notice again that the bearer of the defect is not the producer (the previous author) but an impersonal agency (the data) with Wilson possibly the victim of his data. In this strategy, a defect is reduced to a 'lack' by the author.

Move 3: preview the author's contribution

Until this point in the Introduction, a certain amount of tension has been building up. A particular intellectual area has been defined in Move 1 and a gap within this area has been established. In Move 3, authors declare that they have carried out an investigation in order to close this gap. This move has two main directions; either the authors describe the purpose of the study or they outline the contents of the article. In either case, a deictic marker that points to the author or the present study must be realized. These systems and the realization rules for this act are represented in Figures 3.4. and 3.5. While a minimal unit would suffice (a statement that the research will be presented), Move 3 also allows for great variation in content and in length. The methods, justification for the methods, the hypotheses, and the results may be included.

Changing roles: from narrator to actor

In contrast to the previous moves, the initiation of Move 3 is always signalled by a reference to the authors as producers (*we*, as in [a] below), or their research (*this study*, as in [b] below), which abruptly foregrounds the authors or their present work:

    (a) 'We report here . . .' (Text 5).
    (b) 'The purpose of this study was to . . .' (Text 8).

These selections co-occur with either a statement of the contents or a statement of the purpose of the study. These selections (i.e. System I, Figure 3.4) foreground the authors or their present work. This foregrounding is further reinforced by a change in how authors are referred to. Up to this point, all actors have been referred to in the third person. In fact, when the authors are participants in the earlier narrative (review of literature), they refer to themselves by their surnames or by a third person pronoun. However, in previewing the authors' contribution (Move 3), the syntactic subjects are often the authors (realized by *we*). Myers (1992: 301) proposes that deictic expressions not only serve to distinguish Move 3 from the preceding text but are 'self-referential in the same way as performatives . . .; these expressions work as hereby does in the tests for performative verbs' by pointing to the text as an embodiment of the claim. The use of self-reference shows that the discipline treats the article as an act performed by its publication and its being read. However, while *we* is the agent of verbs such as *suggest, present, report, pose, wish, decide* and *chose*, the research product is the 'agent' for other processes, leading to some anthropomorphism. In research texts, *studies* and not authors have a purpose (*The purpose of this study*

Figure 3.4   A partial system network for features of the head act of Move 3, 'preview author's contribution'

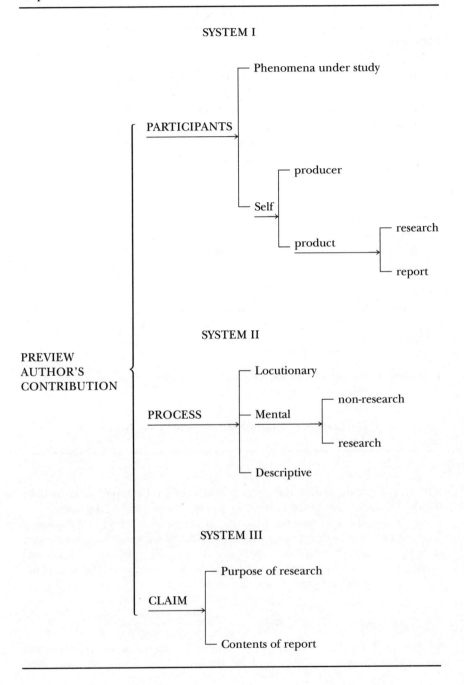

SYSTEM I

PARTICIPANTS
- Phenomena under study
- Self
  - producer
  - product
    - research
    - report

SYSTEM II

PROCESS
- Locutionary
- Mental
  - non-research
  - research
- Descriptive

SYSTEM III

CLAIM
- Purpose of research
- Contents of report

PREVIEW AUTHOR'S CONTRIBUTION

Figure 3.5 Realization rules for features of the head act of Move 3, 'preview author's contribution'

FEATURE	REALIZATION
Participant	
Self	*we* or
product	nominal group representing product of author's research e.g.
research	*study, investigation*
report	*paper, article*
	+identifier: *this, the present* or
	locator: *here*
Process	
Locutionary	*present, report*
Mental	
non-research	*suggest, wish*
research	*examine, measure*
Descriptive	*provide, represent*
Claim	
Purpose of research	lexical item: *purpose*
	infinitive of purpose: *to do X*
Contents of report	name phenomena under study

Examples: 'We report here the results of three studies on one parameter of adult-to-infant speech . . .' (Text 5).
               'We present a replication of the finding of . . .' (Text 4).
               'The purpose of this study was to examine [x phenomenon]' (Text 8).

was . . .). Inanimate entities can also perform high level complex tasks such as: 'Study 3 avoided this problem by . . .', 'Study 3 attempted to disentangle . . .' (Text 15, not in this corpus but from one of the journals found in the corpus). This animation is in direct violation of the APA guidelines (1983: 35, repeated in 1994): 'an experiment cannot attempt to demonstrate, [or] control unwanted variables . . .'; such violations show that the need to submerge the role of the author as actor can override even a stylistic restraint.

Choosing a stance: assertive or modest

In contrast to the foregrounding of the author/actor, the actions attributed to him/her are rather subdued. Authors announce that they will report their findings by means of non-factive verbs, which do not commit them to the truth of the statement that follows. Factive verbs, in contrast, presuppose that the claims which follow are objective fact. For example, authors write *We report here ... * instead of *We have demonstrated that ...* The most frequently chosen verb attributed to the authors in Move 3 is *examine.* In contrast, when authors report the research of others, they do not eschew factive verbs, e.g. *confirm, find, reveal, show, demonstrate, observe.* Only the verbs *report* and *suggest* serve for both the present and previous authors. In addition to selecting non-committal verbs, some social scientists dilute their achievements even further by adding 'tentativity' phrases, such as *we begin to examine, this is a preliminary effort at providing an ... examination.*

On the other hand, it seems misleading to assume that the strength of the claim is established only by the strength of the verb. Strength of claim can be achieved through unhedged statements and adjectives with positive connotations, which may override a non-factive verb (such as *believe* in the following example): 'The present study provides a detailed and systematic description of [x] so that many of these unanswered questions can be addressed. We believe this strategy produced more valid and generalizable results' (Text 3).

Verb selection seems to be very deliberate. For instance, there is some evidence that choice of verb is sensitive to academic field. Firstly, authors of several papers in molecular genetics (Myers, 1992) do not share the hesitancy of social scientists in using factive verbs such as *show, demonstrate* and *find* when presenting their own work. Secondly, Myers' study of 42 papers from the *Journal of Linguistics* reveals a broader range of forms than does molecular biology, using verbs such as *argue, consider, be concerned with, address.* He concludes that choice of verbs confirms that 'these [linguistic] papers seek to persuade their readers of positions, not to report to them some facts' (Myers, 1992: 305). As is common in the humanities, linguistic papers often set out to refute some other interpretation, whereas the choice of *report* (as in 'We report X finding') in biology reflects the idea of findings existing in the real world that are not yet accepted as facts. According to Myers, the fact that certain types of verbs are typically used in each discipline strengthens the relativist argument that scientific knowledge is socially constructed.

Promising to fill the gap

The most salient interpersonal component of Move 3 is that it usually promises to fill the gap established in Move 2. The authors promise either explicitly ('... the present study also examines several fundamental questions that have been neglected' [Text 2] or implicitly by carefully echoing or paraphrasing the gap, as in Move 2: '... these earlier efforts did not consider the possible effects of newscasters' biased facial expressions on voting behaviour ... '. Move 3: 'The two studies reported in this article begin to examine the effects of facial expressions on the part of newscasters' (Text 7).

Authors of ten texts promise to fill the gap in the literature that they have just established. Two texts represent a slight variation in that the authors posit an idealized way to fill the gap, which the present paper presumably will actualize.

Additional examples from the corpus are found in Table 3.2.

In sum, Move 3 is the most formulaic of the three Introductory moves since: (1) it is always signalled (the signalling accomplished by a reference to the authors or their work) and (2) the constituent processes are expressed by a limited number of verbs. Moreover, social scientists tend to prefer verbs which are noncommittal ('This report examines . . .') while molecular biologists are more assertive ('We have demonstrated that . . .'). This difference may reflect the status of proofs in sciences which cannot completely control variables contrasted with laboratory sciences performed under conditions of close control.

Unexpectedly, Move 3 often lacks a statement of hypotheses or research questions. As mentioned above, the only obligatory act is a statement of contents or purpose. Since these types of statements are found in the abstract of the paper, whether implicitly or explicitly, one can question the need for a Move 3, given the constraints on space in journals. It is possible that Move 3 serves a rhetorical rather than an informational function by providing closure to the gap statement by consistently promising to fill the gap.

Distribution and extent of moves

Every text in the present corpus realizes each of the three prototypical moves. However, this is not a necessary condition for 'membership' in the genre. In our view, based on Ventola (1987), a text may 'belong' to a genre even if one or two basic structures are lacking. The omission of these structures is related to other factors in the text; for instance, theoretically, in an entirely new field, it would not be necessary to establish a gap. According to this perspective, given the presence of a certain minimum number of structures, a text is recognizable as a research text, even if, say, the expression of the gap is omitted. Although Ventola refers to the canonical structures as 'obligatory', we prefer to term them 'prototypical' to emphasize that they are expected but not obligatory.

Not only is there a choice of whether or not to realize a certain structure, but the amount of attention afforded to each move is extremely flexible. For instance, the authors of Text 4 devote 92 per cent of the total clauses in the Introduction to establishing relevance (which includes reviewing past literature) while the authors of Text 6 devote the major part (76 per cent of the total clauses) to previewing their own study (Move 3). Similarly, the need to establish a gap can occupy anywhere from 4 per cent to 37 per cent of the Introduction. This variation in length is related to the type of claim: a claim of defects in previous studies requires support, while a claim of scarcity can be realized in one perfunctory clause ('there is no relevant literature').

The variation in proportion of text devoted to each move may carry no rhetorical message, i.e. it may be related to whether the authors have chosen to incorporate their review of previous research into Moves 1, 2 or 3, which in itself may be due to stylistic reasons. Furthermore, some authors choose to

Table 3.2   Realizations of 'promises to fill the gap'

Text Number

A. Explicit promise

3. The present study provides a detailed and systematic description of [x] so that many of these unanswered questions can be addressed. We believe this strategy produced more valid and generalizable results.

B. Implicit promise (Comparisons of 'establish the gap' in Move 2 and 'promise to fill the gap' in Move 3)

1. [MOVE 2 . . . one of its major shortcomings has been its failure to deal with concrete social outcomes such as perceptions of fairness in the distribution of income]

   MOVE 3 Here we measure beliefs about the sources of social inequality and examine their consequences for perceptions of the fairness of income receipts.

4. [MOVE 2 Since that time, there have been no further reports on the association between thought disorder and eye-movement abnormalities.]

   MOVE 3 We present a replication of the finding of an association between thought disorder and eye-tracking dysfunctions.

6. [MOVE 2 Little attention has been focused on factors that may predict children's social and school adjustment during this period.]

   MOVE 3 The primary purpose of this study was to explore the transition from preschool to kindergarten and to identify factors that predict children's social function and school adjustment in the new classroom environment.

C. Positing of an idealized way to fill the gap which the present paper presumably will actualize

9. [ideal] The lack of research in this area is not accidental. The design requirements for such a systematic examination are stringent and difficult to meet.

   [promise] The present paper represents a preliminary effort at providing such an examination.

12. [ideal] What is needed is a study in which a number of facial expressions are manipulated, and a number of feelings measured.

    [promise – implied] Because the most likely candidate for a single dimension is the unpleasantness dimension, we decided to use only negative emotions.

---

discuss hypotheses, and even results, in Move 3 while others omit these two elements (resulting in a very short Move 3). However, a rhetorical explanation sees such 'arbitrary' decisions as a means of highlighting the importance of this work for human welfare or research (Move 1) or emphasizing the extent of missing information in the field (Move 2). This last choice may reflect the need to fit new research into a very crowded field, or one dominated by certain classics which have blocked the introduction of fresh concepts into the field. In sum, although the three moves are prototypical for the genre, the amount of text devoted to each move is at the author's discretion and tends to reflect how the author is situating the article in the research field.

Sequence of moves

One of the questions that must be addressed in genre analysis is the prototypical sequencing of moves. That is, part of the realization of a social process is through the order in which communicative structures occur. Chapter 1 reports two basic approaches to the question of sequencing. Hasan (Halliday and Hasan, 1985) argues that canonical ordering of elements is one criterion for determining whether texts are valid instances of the genre.

In the other view (Ventola, 1987), ordering is the result of a series of decisions. Ventola's view of text creation is more dynamic, allowing for decisions at every step of the creation of the text, rather than a compulsory filling in of pre-determined slots. Although Ventola based her view on oral exchanges, this concept seems especially pertinent to written text, where re-reading can correct any misinterpretation produced by non-canonical ordering. In Introduction sections of research texts, although the majority adhere to the canonical sequence, i.e.

1. claim relevance of field;
2. establish the gap the present research is meant to fill; and
3. preview the authors' contribution,

an author can decide to lead with Move 2 (gap) or Move 3 (preview) and still present a coherent report, acceptable as a member of the genre. In the non-canonical ordering some extra signals of transitions and discourse structure may be necessary.

These findings about the order of moves (1. relevance, 2. gap and 3. preview) contrast with a frequently cited, earlier study on social science texts. Crookes (1986: 65) reports that no social science texts present Moves 1, 2, 3 in this linear sequence. Since we used texts from the same journals, this inconsistency in findings is most probably due to the difference between the method of coding used in Crookes' study and in the present study; for example, Crookes did not specify the extent of a move; see our discussion of linguistic units in Chapter 2.

A second question related to ordering is whether gaps (Move 2) can be reported in 'composite' form, i.e. as a general statement at the end of a literature review, or in cyclical form, i.e. each gap following a review of a particular variable, so that cycles composed of Move 1 and Move 2 recur. In Swales' (1990) study, social science texts more often followed the cyclical pattern while physical science texts conformed to the composite pattern. He speculates that it is likely that:

> choice [composite vs. cyclical form] is influenced by how the research field is perceived. If the relevant research tradition is viewed as linear and cumulative, then a composite arrangement may work well. However, if the field is viewed as branching – consisting of several loosely connected topics – then a cyclic approach may be preferred. (p. 158)

However, in the present corpus of social science texts, the major pattern is that of a composite gap, e.g. 'Although facial expressions of newscasters have been studied in the past, these earlier efforts did not consider the possible effects of newscasters' facial expressions on voting behaviour' (Text 7).

In only three texts, a cyclical pattern occurs, i.e. Moves 1 and 2 are recursive 1, ([1, 2], [1, 2]) 3, where the first element establishes relevance for a general phenomenon and each of the bracketed segments establishes the relevance and gap for a specific variable within that phenomenon. An explanation of the choice of compositeness or cycles as a reflection of differences in academic fields ('branching out' versus 'linearity') awaits confirmation.

On the other hand, in the next section, we permit ourselves to speculate as to the reasons these particular three moves evolved and are sequenced as they are. We have already implied that, viewed separately, each move is superfluous; Move 1 conveys no new information to the expert; Move 2 ('establish the gap') is dispensed with in some academic fields, and Move 3 can be succinctly expressed as a metacomment: 'We present a report of study x . . .'.

Introductions as narratives

It is possible, however, that moves in Introductions evolved from a narrative schema (as did the entire research text): chronological, general to specific, background to foreground. As mentioned in Chapter 1, the earliest research article in English (in the *Philosophical Transactions of the Royal Society of London*) was a brief narrative, reported as a news story (Bazerman, 1987a). In its contemporary form, a research text weaves two strands of ideational material together: (1) a strand about certain facts (static in time) in the physical world is reported within (2) a research narrative about the uncovering of these facts, which takes place within the social world of the research community. The research narrative often unfolds chronologically with appropriate markers: *early/classical/past/previous/recent*. The time indicators terminate after the narrative arrives at *present research*.

In the oral narrative genre, the elements are *orientation* or *setting*, *corpus* and *coda*. The initial element locates the story in time and introduces the participants (Link, 1978; Schottelndreyer, 1978; Labov and Waletzky, 1967). As *setting* in narratives orients the reader in physical space and time, relevance in scientific texts orients the reader in intellectual space by establishing the time frame (timeless or at least current) and naming the participants (research products and producers, human populations, and variables under study). In examining narratives, Labov and Waletzky (1967) expanded the *corpus* element to *complication, resolution* and *evaluation.*

Complication introduces a problematic state; this element can be compared to the state of tension produced in Move 2, e.g. 'A final concern with studies of tobacco withdrawal is that several important facets of the disorder have not been well described' (Text 3). *Resolution* consists of the remainder of the text but its precursor is the announcement (comparable to our Move 3) that resolution will follow, as in 'The present study provides a detailed and systematic description of tobacco withdrawal so that many of these unanswered questions can be addressed' (Text 3). We will later, in the Discussion section, find a statement that the complication has been resolved, as in 'In summary, the present study clarified several aspects of tobacco withdrawal' (Text 3).

The parallel between folk tales and scientific texts has been previously commented upon by Grimes (1975). To parallel Grimes' terminology, Move 1 can be likened to the *equilibrium* state, in which an accepted fact in the academic community is asserted, e.g. 'Major changes in work and leisure activities . . . have occurred in the US in the last few decades' (Text 1). The equilibrium state continues with minor characters (other researchers) as performers. The major activities, performed by the narrator/actor, commence with Move 3 in which the authors now take over the narrative. This juncture is often marked by foregrounding the new participant, e.g. 'We report here the results of three studies . . .' (Text 5).

The remainder of the research text can also be seen as analogous to the narrative schema, as is discussed in Chapter 8.

Summary

In sum, Introductions are distinguished by three generic structures (moves):

1. 'claim relevance of field', in which the authors justify their choice of phenomena for intensive study;
2. 'establish the gap the present research is meant to fill', in which the authors point out that the knowledge about the subject they have chosen is incomplete; and
3. 'preview the authors' contribution', in which the authors proclaim that they have tried to fill the gap.

All three structures are common to all texts in the corpus; the majority appear in the linear order of Moves 1, 2, 3. On the other hand, authors enjoyed considerable latitude in the amount of text they chose to devote to each move; i.e. authors can emphasize Move 1, 2 or 3.

A system for generating realizations of each move is provided. Within the realization of these elements, however, authors can exercise many options that reflect the interpersonal dimension. Within the realization for Move 1, several prerogatives can be exercised. For one, the claim of relevance (Move 1) may be based on the value of the present study in furthering the understanding of human behaviour or in augmenting research but tends to be directed to the former value. Secondly, Move 1 must be mapped onto either a general field or a specific phenomenon within that field; the trend is to map it onto the more general field. Similarly, although 'establish the gap' (Move 2) must be realized, its form is very flexible. Establishing the gap can vary from enumerating defects in specific previous studies to stating that, generally, certain factors are unknown. This option and the third option, a claim of scarcity ('Literature on the phenomenon is rare') need not be substantiated by literature citations. Hence, statements that establish the gap can use various techniques to avoid direct criticisms of specific researchers.

Move 3 (a very short preview of what the article will disclose), in contrast to the other two moves, is formulaic even in the choice of processes ('In this article, we report . . .'). The most salient component of Move 3 is that it usually promises to fill the gap established in Move 2.

Some of the features and the ordering of the moves seem to be analogous to those of a narrative schema and a problem solution schema (chronological, general to specific, background to foreground).

Notes

1. The term **relevance** was not chosen in order to reflect the concept of relevance offered by Sperber and Wilson (1986); however, there is some overlap in both our uses of the term. Sperber and Wilson's concept of relevance is applicable to the total text, while we use it to designate a particular structure within the text. The term relevance seems less value-laden than other possible terms such as *importance, significance* or *worthwhileness*.
2. The ecological analogy was suggested by Swales (1990: 141) who examined a wide range of fields and designated the moves in Introductions as: Move 1, Establishing a Territory; Move 2, Establishing a Niche; and Move 3, Occupying the Niche.

4 Inviting applause: analysis of Discussion sections

Introduction

In this chapter, we focus on an analysis of prototypical moves in Discussion sections, following the same methodology (outlined in Chapter 2) as that for Introduction sections of research texts; we also list component acts, and provide system networks from which the realizations of head acts can be generated. This follows from the definition and discussion in Chapter 2 of generic structures in terms of their realization in the discourse units of moves and acts. Moves are composed of at least one obligatory act (the head) and slots for optional acts (pre-head and post-head).

Before examining the moves in our Discussion sections, it is relevant to recall the inconsistencies in definitions and lack of common units of analysis in the current research on Discussion sections; the number of moves varied from three (Nwogu, 1997) to eleven (Peng, 1987); see Chapter 2. Only one move, summarizing results, was common to most studies. At present, there is no way to determine whether these differences result from the differences in academic field studied or from the lack of uniform definitions and common units of analysis, a problem that we have discussed before and that we will address again here in relation to the Discussion section. We suggest that a more consistent approach to the identification and description of moves is available if moves are defined in terms of their communicative purposes, such as we have demonstrated in outlining the moves in Introductions. As mentioned earlier, the primary rhetorical functions of research texts are: Introduction, Methods, Results and Discussion. In examining our data, we found that Discussion sections of research texts could be described in terms of five secondary rhetorical functions (moves). Each move realized one or more component acts, i.e. rhetorical functions at a lower (tertiary) rank. Thus, these five moves included all the acts in the corpus. These prototypical moves are:

A. report accomplishments;
B. evaluate congruence of findings to other criteria;
C. offer interpretation;
D. ward off counterclaims;
E. state implications.

The key moves

In this section, we provide a brief definition and example for each move; in order to construct definitions that will be applicable across disciplines, we establish realizational criteria, which we explain in the following section. In the third section, 'Embedding the authors' aims in the key moves', we discuss the options within each move.

Definitions

Move A: REPORT ACCOMPLISHMENTS: in the head act, *report findings*, authors express in more general terms the quantitative relationships between variables they have found in the present study (which have been previously reported under the Results section),[1] as for example 'In the studies we have reported here, the extent of FM of an auditory stimulus *per se* was not effective in specially maintaining infants' visual attention' (Text 5).

After basically repeating their results, the authors apply some qualitative yardstick to them. They may assess their study by comparing the methods or results to hypotheses, methods, results of other studies or to general criteria for research. We have termed this: Move B: EVALUATE CONGRUENCE OF FINDINGS WITH OTHER CRITERIA. We consider Move B a separate move, rather than an act supporting ACCOMPLISHMENTS, because it can appear independently of Move A. One of the more modest examples of Move B is 'In sum, the unexpected effects of expressions were in every case consistent with other research on the dimensional structure and similarity among emotions' (Text 12).

After measuring the aptness of the present research, an explanation is called for. In Move C: OFFER INTERPRETATION, the key act is *offer hypothesis*, which we define here as a claim, endorsed by the authors, suggesting why or how the phenomena under study are or should be related, as in 'Perhaps the reason why children with more extensive patterns of positive contacts tended to receive . . . was that they had established a history of . . .' (Text 6). This definition is supported by Kerlinger (1973: 9): '. . . a theory explains phenomena . . . by specifying what variables are related to what variables and how they are related'.

But the authors recognize that others may see defects in their methods or posit different explanations for the results. Therefore, in the next move, D, the authors WARD OFF COUNTERCLAIMS.

This move, unlike the others, has two obligatory elements: *raise potential counterclaims* and *respond to the counterclaims*. Counterclaims include the possibility of deficiencies in the present methods or interpretations other than the authors', e.g. 'While the issue of procedural sensitivity may be raised in the context of these negative findings . . .' (Text 5). Responding can be accomplished by either of the following options:

a. accepting responsibility:
   'Thus, the lack of predictive findings regarding . . . may be due to our failure to evaluate how . . .' (Text 1) or

    b. dismissing counterclaims by:
- (1) citing findings, as in 'However, an inspection of children's sociometric nomination ... [finding] failed to support the latter interpretation' (Text 6);
- (2) justifying methods, or evaluating congruence, as in 'In our interviews, an effort was made to minimize problems with context effect by ...' (Text 8); or
- (3) speculating (i.e. positing a refuting hypothesis), as in Text 5, below.

A text could reasonably end at this point but most authors prefer to discuss the implications of their study for the future (Move E: STATE IMPLICA-TIONS). The purpose of the head act may be any one of the following:

1. to recommend continued research on the variables under study, e.g. '... future research on these issues will be more successful to the extent that it addresses the social psychological meaning of ...' (Text 1).
2. to recommend a change in the theoretical stance of the discipline, e.g. '... the current theoretical approaches to [x] may need to be reexamined' (Text 8).
3. to recommend changes in social policy to reflect the results of the study, e.g. 'The findings from the present study raise important implications for researchers and educators interested in the prevention of ... difficulties' (Text 6). (Remainder of move specifies implications for educators only.)

The move, 'stating implications' may realize one, two, or all types of implications above. Also, it may realize more than one of each type of implication.

Component acts

As we have seen, a move is composed of at least one obligatory act (the head) and slots for optional acts (pre-head and post-head). The result is that the components of instantiated moves can be different from each other. Table 4.1 illustrates possible component acts of the moves in Discussion sections.

In addition to the acts listed in Table 4.1, there are several other types of acts which appear less frequently in one of the five moves:

1. (re)assert relevance:
   'Several changes in the opportunity structure and activity patterns in the United States have taken place in recent years ...' (Text 2)
2. claim that purpose has been realized:
   'In summary, the present study ... clarified several aspects of tobacco withdrawal ...' (Text 3)
3. (re)assert gaps in literature which existed prior to the present research:
   'Most of these models do not postulate precisely how ...' (Text 8)
4. offer comments:
   '... we are encouraged by the viability and meaningfulness of the results' (Text 9)

Table 4.1 Component acts of 'moves' in Discussion sections of research texts

MOVE A	REPORT ACCOMPLISHMENTS

Example structure:

Pre-head:	**announce that findings will follow:** 'In this study . . . we found many similarities as well as several differences between the sexes.'
Head:	**report findings:** 'Our data revealed that the women we studied generally began using cocaine at a younger age than men' (Text 10).

MOVE B	EVALUATE CONGRUENCE OF FINDINGS WITH OTHER CRITERIA

Example structure:

Head (one or more):	**express superiority of present research to past research** **express consistency with past research** **express inconsistency with past research** **express consistency with hypothesis**
Post-head:	**give specifications of past research**

MOVE C	OFFER INTERPRETATION

Example structure:

Pre-head:	**announce that interpretation will follow:** 'In contrast with patients with affective disorders, the coupling of eye-movement dysfunctions and thought disorder in schizophrenic patients can be explained differently.'
Pre-head:	**report what is known about general phenomenon under study:** 'The central nervous system disorder suggested by eye-tracking impairments . . . represents a hypothesized latent trail.'
Head:	**offer hypothesis:** 'The results of the present study suggest that thought disorder in schizophrenics may be another manifestation of this latent trait.'
Post-head:	**claim support for hypothesis:** 'This formulation is supported by the evidence that . . .' (Text 4).

Table 4.1 Component acts of 'moves' in Discussion sections of research texts (*continued*)

MOVE D	WARD OFF COUNTERCLAIMS

Example structure:

Head:	**A. raise counterclaim**
	B. respond: dismiss
	(1) evaluate congruence
	(2) report findings
Post-head:	**offer conclusion**
	(For example see Text 5, below)

MOVE E	STATE IMPLICATIONS

Example structure:

Pre-head:	**review methods**
Pre-head:	**speculate**
Head:	**recommend further research**
Post-head:	**justify recommendation**
	(For examples, see Text 5, below)
Post-head:	**promise to carry out recommendations:**
	'The logical next step in research would be . . . We are currently engaged in such a program of investigation' (Text 9).

5. state metacomments:
   'Three aspects of this outcome require discussion . . .' (Text 4).

The text below illustrates three moves and component acts within a complete Discussion text. (Text 5 was chosen for this purpose because of its brevity.)

MOVE A – REPORT ACCOMPLISHMENTS

[**report finding**] 'in the studies we have reported here, the extent of FM of an auditory stimulus *per se* was not effective in specially maintaining infants' visual attention.
[**comment**] It does not seem reasonable, therefore, to attribute the salience of motherese to young infants to this parameter alone.

MOVE D – WARD OFF COUNTERCLAIMS

[**A. raise potential counterclaim**] While the issue of procedural sensitivity may be raised in the context of these negative findings,

[B. respond]
[evaluate congruence] the visual fixation paradigms used in this series of studies have been shown in the past to be sensitive to infants' selective attentional responses to auditory stimuli [Names].
[report finding] Furthermore, infants' attention to stimuli in Experiment 1 was sufficient to allow readily observable discrimination.
[offer conclusion] If the salience of a stimulus parameter is observable only within certain procedural constraints . . . the parameter cannot be considered to be a powerful one. The consistency of the results across the two techniques and three different stimuli employed in these studies suggests this to be the case.
[comment] Given the pervasiveness of exaggerated intonation or modulation patterns in adult-to-infant speech, these negative results become all the more interesting.

MOVE E – STATE IMPLICATIONS

[review methods] We have manipulated one of a number of possible stimulus parameters present in adult-to-infant speech.
[speculate] The possibility exists that, within the context of or in combination with other such parameters . . . frequency modulation might serve as an alerting or signalling cue for infants to attend to speech.
[recommend research] The attribution of infant selectivity to such configurations of auditory parameters remains to be more directly investigated.
[justify recommendation] Such a demonstration would raise important issues regarding the ecological validity of studying the acoustic factors of speech in isolation' (Text 5).
(Reproduced with the kind permission of the Society for Research in Child Development, Inc.)

We have focused on the first step in the characterization of research texts by defining moves by their communicative purposes. The next step is to arrive at realization criteria for each move. We review our method below and examine realizational criteria for two moves, Move C, 'offer interpretation', and Move E, 'state implications', in detail.

How are moves realized in texts?

Defining a move by its communicative purpose is a necessary but not sufficient condition for assigning moves to categories. The following text illustrates the problem; adjacent sentences A and B clearly express different purposes and therefore can be assigned to different moves, which we later labelled, respectively, *report accomplishments* and *offer interpretation*:

A. 'Although our observations confirm that boys and girls are receiving similar instructions about sex-types toys, they also indicate that parents show affective differences in their reactions to boys' and girls' choices of sex-typed behaviour.'

B. 'It appears that the sex-role education of boys and girls is differentiated on the basis of affective response, rather than cognitive information' (Text 11).

In this case, we tentatively assign (B) to the category 'hypothesis' because it selects for uncertainty ('It appears') and makes a claim about the relationship between variables '[x] is differentiated on the basis of [y]'.

But how can we account for varying realizations of *offer interpretation* in different texts?

1. 'It appears that the sex-role education of boys and girls is differentiated on the basis of affective response, rather than cognitive information' (Text 11).
2. 'The first general explanation holds that the newscaster bias had a causal effect on viewer attitudes, and we consider this explanation to be the most plausible one' (Text 7).
3. 'Thus, some of the symptoms of tobacco withdrawal may be due to frustration rather than nicotine deprivation' (Text 3).
4. 'Nonetheless, it is quite clear that social resources play a dominating role in buffering social-psychological stress in the life stress process when physical health is the outcome variable of concern' (Text 9).
5. 'The present study suggests that exposure to stress can trigger enduring changes in mental health' (Text 8).

Although 1–5 share a purpose, they do not share a lexeme or a grammatical feature, such as modals of *uncertainty*. As we have indicated in Chapter 2, in order to arrive at uniform realization criteria, we propose semantic categories, specifying the kinds of participants and processes necessary in order to realize different acts. For instance, analysis of all the realizations of *offer interpretation* in the corpus reveals that they choose their elements from the classes represented in Figure 4.1. The categories can be expanded if additional classes are found in future corpora. Realization rules, as in Figure 4.2, then stipulate which of the features from the system network are chosen when other conditions hold (i.e. when a particular act is chosen from another level of the generation of the research article).

The realization criteria for the head act of *offer interpretation* are specified below. To recall, we defined this move as one in which the authors explain why the phenomena under study are or should be related.

The minimal criteria for *offer hypothesis* (the head act of *offer interpretation*), shared by the four variants, above, are:

a. the authors refer to themselves or their present research, represented in System I [Producer]. This reference may be realized in the previous move, *report accomplishments*: [*Our observations* . . . (Text 11)] which establishes that the subsequent claim is theirs;
b. the phenomena under study are named (System I);
c. an expression of a relationship between the two phenomena is realized, i.e. [Relation] is chosen (System II in Figure 4.1). This is one of the contrasting features to 'evaluate congruence', e.g. 'We believe the validity

of our results is greater than that of prior studies for several reasons' (Text 3);

d. the stance [Conjecture] is realized (System III), expressed as intellectual conjecture (*it appears, explanation, it is quite clear*) OR as tentativity in the physical world (*X may be due to Y*). Modals of uncertainty cannot be a defining feature. Although they co-occur with the majority of instances of 'offering an interpretation' this is not always true, as in 'The causal mechanism for this explanation must involve the subtle operation of . . .' (Text 7).

Although in the examples given below, most features are realized in one sentence, this is not always the case. Part of the realization may occur in a pre-head structure such as 'There are three possible explanations for these results'.

This approach captures the commonality of the moves in all the realizations in our corpus.

The last two criteria, [Relation] and [Conjecture], are highlighted, by underlining and boldface, respectively, in the following examples:

1. '**It appears** that the sex-role education of boys and girls <u>is differentiated on the basis of</u> affective response, rather than cognitive information' (Text 11).
2. 'The first general **explanation** holds that the newscaster bias <u>had a causal effect</u> on viewer attitudes, and we consider this explanation <u>to be</u> the most plausible one' (Text 7).
3. 'Thus, some of the symptoms of tobacco withdrawal **may be** <u>due to</u> frustration rather than nicotine deprivation' (Text 3).
4. 'Nonetheless, **it is quite clear that** social resources <u>play a dominating role in buffering</u> social-psychological stress in the life stress process when physical health is the outcome variable of concern' (Text 9).
5. 'The present study **suggests** that exposure to stress <u>can trigger enduring changes</u> in mental health' (Text 8).

Using the metadiscoursal comment/frame alone would lead to misclassification as shown in the two texts below which have a similar container sentence as a frame:

1. 'There are several possible explanations for the poor performance of [x] variables in explaining . . . However, [explanation dismissed]' (Text 2 – Move D – ward off counterclaims).
2. 'There are three possible explanations for these results . . . The first general explanation holds that the newscaster bias had a causal effect on viewer attitudes, and we consider this explanation to be the most plausible one' (Text 7 – Move C – offer interpretation).

Thus, the choice of the claim bearer structure 'an explanation /is/' instead of 'producers [we] claim . . .' can be a prelude to either a dismissal of a counterclaim or an acceptance of an interpretation and cannot be relied upon as a defining feature.

Figure 4.1 A partial system network for features of the head act of Move C, 'offer interpretation'

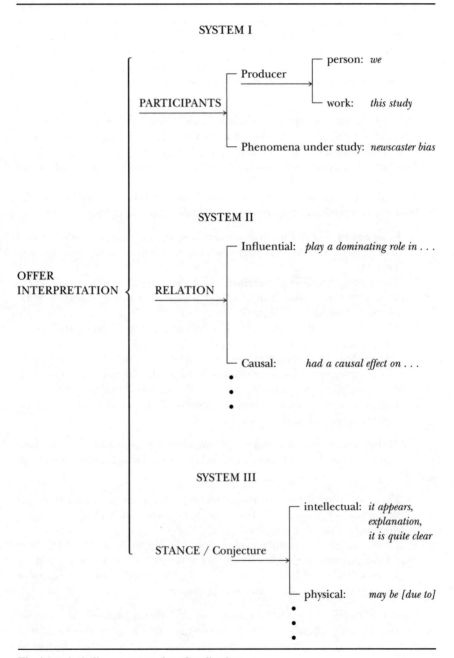

The items in italics are examples of realizations.

Figure 4.2 Realization rules for the head act of Move C, 'offer interpretation'

FEATURE	REALIZATION
	ENDORSEMENT STRUCTURE
Participants	
Producer	
person	authors: *we*
work	identifier + research product: *the present study*
Stance:	
Conjecture	epistemic modality in e.g.
intellectual (1)	verbal group: *suggest* or nominal group: *explanation*
	HYPOTHESIS STRUCTURE
Participants:	
Phenomena under study	(context dependent)
Relation	attribute or process of phenomena under study:
Causal	*a causal effect*
Influential	*play a dominating role*
Stance:	
Conjecture	epistemic modality in modal operator: *may, must*
physical (2)	lexical verb: *appear, suggest* adjective: *possible* noun: *possibility* adverb: *perhaps*

Conjecture can be realized as either (1) or (2).

The items in italics are examples of realizations.

Examples: 'The first general explanation holds that the newscaster bias had a causal effect onviewer attitudes [HYPOTHESIS STRUCTURE: RELATION = CAUSAL], and we consider this explanation to be the most plausible one' [ENDORSEMENT STRUCTURE] (Text 7).

'The significance of these findings can now be recast . . . in the proposed conceptual model [ENDORSEMENT STRUCTURE]. . . . it is quite clear that social resources play a dominating role in buffering social-psychological stress in the life stress process . . .' [HYPOTHESIS STRUCTURE: RELATION = INFLUENTIAL] (Text 9).

Move E: state implications

Since 'recommend research' is the head act in more than half of the instances of Move E, we will focus on its realizations in more detail. Three examples of the realizations of 'recommend research' in this corpus are shown below:

'. . . future research on these issues will be more successful to the extent that it addresses the social-psychological meaning of . . .' (Text 1).

'The attribution of infant selectivity to such configurations of auditory parameters remains to be more directly investigated' (Text 5).

'The logical next step in research would be an empirical investigation of the conceptual model . . .' (Text 9).

As we have shown with *offer interpretation*, there is clearly a common communicative purpose to these acts, in this case, to propose the research that should be done next. But because of the variation in realizations we need to determine features that will capture these diverse types of stating recommendations. Moves (and the acts within moves) cannot always be identified by their location within the text, although Implications must be located within the Discussion section. Similarly, lexicogrammatical features cannot identify all instances of this move. The most likely candidate, a modal of recommendation, such as 'should' or 'need to', fails to materialize in 75 per cent of the realizations of Move E. Similarly, an explicit lexical signal of futurity such as *future/subsequent* research is not common to all. Furthermore, relying upon futurity as an identification criterion would allow sentences such as 'Money is needed for future research' to be classified as a recommendation for research.

A more valid approach for identification of moves must be based on meaning rather than specific surface structures. Semantic criteria capture the common meaning of the propositions, even when it is realized by various grammatical classes, syntactic structures, and lexemes.

We can see from the examples above (and the remainder in our corpus) that the various realizations can all be reduced to the proposition: *The research that is advisable to do next is [field of inquiry]*. All of the recommendations, including the three diverse realizations shown at the beginning of this section, incorporate these three obligatory semantic categories:

a. 'research' (in upper case letters) – whether realized as a product of research (e.g. 'study') or as an activity of research (e.g. 'investigated');
b. a (proposed) focus of inquiry (underlined);
c. advisability (bold) – realized by inadequacy as a current property of research or field of inquiry as in: [X] focus of inquiry **remains to be** . . ., **needs**, **requires**, **rests on**, **must be**, **should be investigated**; or by desirability as a property of potential research or field of inquiry such as: [X] research [be] **successful**, **essential**, **important**, **useful**, **worthwhile**.

Figure 4.3 A partial system network for features of the head act of Move E 'recommend research'

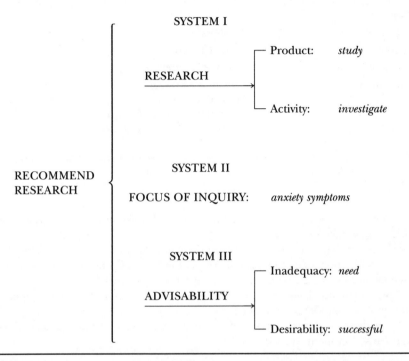

The items in italics are examples of realizations.

The examples below illustrate how these criteria can be applied:

Text 1 ... future RESEARCH on these issues will be more **successful** to the extent that it addresses the social-psychological meaning of ...
Text 5. The attribution of infant selectivity to such configurations ... **remains to be** more directly INVESTIGATED.
Text 9. The **logical** next step in RESEARCH would be an empirical investigation of the conceptual model ...

The system networks shown in Figure 4.3 display the necessary features for recommending research, Move E. The realization rules are depicted in Figure 4.4.

Some of the features of 'recommend research' may be common to other acts. Although the following statements realize the semantic classes (a) research and (c) advisability, they do not qualify as 'recommend research' since they lack (b) the focus of inquiry; they should be considered metadiscoursal comments (pre-head).

Figure 4.4   Realization rules for the head act of Move E, 'state implications'

FEATURE	REALIZATION
Research:	
product	nominal group: *test*
activity	verbal group: *investigate*
Focus of Inquiry	[names of phenomena]
Advisability	attribute of research: realized by:
	adjective: *essential*
	nominal group: *a challenge*
	verbal group: *needs to be devoted*

Example: ... *longer term investigations* [Research] *may be essential* [Advisability] *for a full appreciation of the impact* ... [Focus of Inquiry] (Text 8).

'However, four major issues surrounding . . . theories of victimization warrant further investigation' (Text 2).

'These findings suggest a number of directions for future research' (Text 8).

We have stipulated realizational criteria for Moves C and E in detail, above. System networks and realization rules for the remaining moves are discussed below. The network and realization rules for Move A, 'report accomplishments', are displayed in Figures 4.5 and 4.6.

Lest these be thought of as static systems, the degree of latitude each allows is discussed in the next section.

Embedding the author's aims in the key moves

The five moves in the Discussion section are driven by varying degrees of interpersonal exigencies; at one end of the continuum is *report accomplishments*, which centres on existential reality (what the authors found), while at the other end, *ward off counterclaims* and, to a lesser degree, *state implications* are based on subjective and interpersonal considerations. *Ward off counterclaims* can be said to have been created solely to deal with the relations between writer and reader, in this case, scientist and colleagues. Move B, *evaluate congruence*, allows for varying degrees of judgement about the 'fitness' of one's claims/conclusions. We examine these moves in detail below.

Move B: evaluate congruence of findings with other criteria

As stated above, authors evaluate by comparing methods or results of their study to their hypotheses (as in 1, below), or to criteria external to this research (as in 2, below), such as the methods or results of other studies, or to existing standards for research (as in 3, below).

Figure 4.5   A partial system network for features of the head act of Move A, 'report accomplishments'

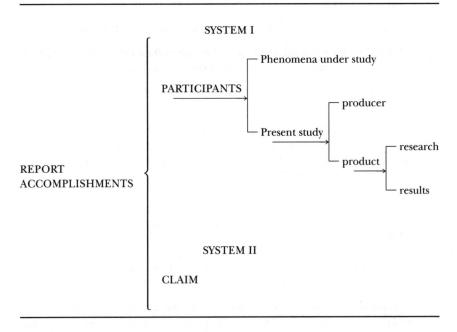

Figure 4.6   Realization rules for features of the head act of Move A, 'report accomplishments'

FEATURE	REALIZATION
Participant	
Present study	Source of results: realized by:
producer	*we* or absence of human agent, or
product	nominal group representing product of author's research + identifier, e.g.
research	*this study/investigation* or
results	*the results/data/Table x*
Claim	Describe end states of phenomena under study

Example: 'The results [RESULTS + IDENTIFIER] of posture are parallel to those of the facial expressions. In both cases, the subjects . . . reported [x]' [CLAIM] (Text 12).

1. 'This finding is consistent with the hypothesis that . . .' (Text 6)
2. '. . . these results are consistent with the view expressed by [N] (1974) that . . .' (Text 8).

Results can also be congruent with both internal and external criteria, as in:

3. 'These results emerged both on previously validated . . . scales and on measures designed especially for this project' (Text 8).

With 'congruence' as the base line, authors project varying degrees of self confidence:

4. Present results can be superior (i.e. more than just 'congruent') to previous work, e.g. 'We believe the validity of our results is greater than that of prior studies for several reasons . . . We also believe the results of our study are more generalizable than those of prior retrospective surveys . . . to our knowledge, the present study is the first to document observable changes . . .' (Text 3).
   'The present finding that . . . fills an obvious gap in the literature . . .' (Text 9).
5. Present results can be less than congruent, as in 'Although these results are somewhat contradictory to those of Weinraub *et al.* (1984), [our children were almost a year younger . . .]' (Text 11).

The systems are depicted in Figure 4.7. As the realizational criteria show (Figure 4.8), in this move, authors compare their present research to existing standards, according to attributes of goodness (such as *reliability*), agreement (*consistent with other research*), or completeness.

Move D: ward off counterclaims

Presumably, in the past, when the author reported research in the presence of potential critics, the response was immediate and actual as this extract attests:

> In a communication . . . that was read before the Royal Society, January 8, 1863, I brought forward experimental evidence which had conducted me to view the immunity . . . The opposition that this view received on the evening of its announcement induced me to extend my experiments, and . . . I have deemed it desirable to present this further communication, in which the whole subject is concisely reviewed with the aid of the new matter that has been brought to light. (Valle, 1997: 92)

In today's texts, the move 'ward off counterclaims' may be a vestige of such events as described above, transformed into an imaginary dialogue between the author and projected critics. In this move, authors avoid the creation of a new gap (in addition to that established in Move 2 in the Introduction section) by anticipating potential criticism by the audience, and then neutralizing it, either by dismissing it or accepting responsibility. (The options for both elements are shown in Figures 4.9 and 4.11.) Somewhere between acceptance and dismissal is a non-committal stance that can best be called **acknowledgment**, as in:

Figure 4.7 A partial system network for features of the head act of Move B, 'evaluate congruence'

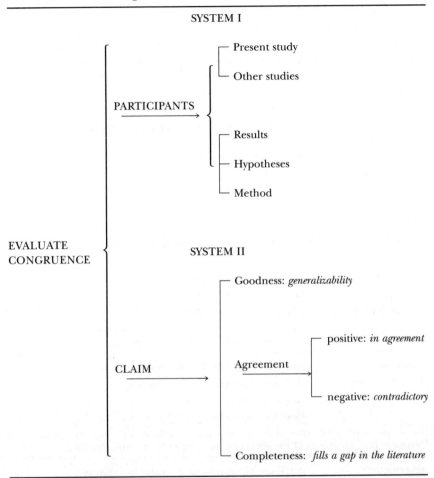

The items in italics are examples of realizations.

'There is no way to rule out this possibility definitively' (Text 7). Although 'raise' and 'respond' are two elements, they can be conflated when the authors raise a counterclaim and 'accept' by not responding, as in: 'One limitation of this study is . . .' (Text 10).

In 'raise potential counterclaims', the 'critic' can be the author, as in 'There are several possible explanations for the poorer performance of [x variables] in explaining violent victimization. First, . . . our aggregate measure . . . may have suppressed the impact of [x] variables' (Text 2). However, the usual 'critic' is an unknown third party ('**One** could try to make the case that . . .' Text 7).

Figure 4.8 Realization rules for features of the head act of Move B, 'evaluate congruence'

FEATURE	REALIZATION
Participants:	
Present study	EVALUATED: realized by nominal group representing research + identifier as self, e.g. *this study/investigation* or
Findings	*the/these results/data*
	CRITERIA: realized by
Other studies	nominal group representing research + identifier as other, e.g.
	other/prior research or
Findings	*those results/data* or
	present study: hypotheses
	present study: method
Claim	
Goodness	positive research trait: *reliability, validity*
Agreement	
positive	similarity: *replicable, consistent*
negative	lack of similarity: *not common*
Completeness:	*fills a gap in the literature*

Variation A:	An aspect of present study is superior to criteria
Goodness:	Attribute of present study; and/or
	deficient attribute of other studies
Example:	'We believe the validity of our results is greater than that of prior studies for several reasons' (Text 3)

Variation B:	An aspect of present study is in agreement with criteria
Agreement: positive	Attribute of present study and other studies
Examples:	'In sum, the unexpected effects of expressions were in every case consistent with other research . . .' (Text 12).
	'Although the results fit the general multidimensional expectations quite nicely . . .' (Text 12).

Variation C:	An aspect of present study is not in agreement with criteria
Agreement: negative	Attribute of present study or of criteria
Example:	'Although these results are somewhat contradictory to those of W . . .' (Text 11).

Acceptance can be **wholehearted**, when the authors name themselves as perpetrators of the mistake, as they do in only one instance in the corpus: 'Thus the lack of predictive findings regarding ... may be due to our failure to evaluate how ...' (Text 1). In that study, the authors have to account for the fact that their hypotheses were not confirmed. Contrary to expectations, the choice of [CRITIC: Self] does not predict that the authors will accept the criticism, as is shown in 'In our judgement, the most serious threat to the validity of these findings concerns the possibility that R's ...' (text continues to dismiss this claim) (Text 8). In contrast, acceptance can be **fainthearted**, when the authors admit a mistake, but fail to identify themselves as the perpetrators, as in 'One limitation of this study is the fact that it took place at a single institution ...' (Text 10).

Accepting responsibility can also be diffused by various degrees of mitigation. The more usual approach is to mitigate one's culpability by projecting, i.e. blaming an extraneous factor, such as problems inherent in the variables, as in 'In their present form, routine activities ... theories are basically unfalsifiable since ...' (Text 2).

A factor in the method may also be blamed, e.g. 'These contradictory results may be due to the limited generalizability of sleep laboratory studies or to ...' (Text 3). Alternatively, the authors may rationalize away the difficulty. To do so, they simultaneously admit there may have been a deficiency in their methods and protest that it would probably not have made a difference, as shown by 'Although it is unlikely that withdrawal symptoms would influence long-term abstinence, a prospective study of the influence of withdrawal symptoms on ... would have been a much better test than the present study' (Text 3).

Just as there are many possible degrees of accepting responsibility, dismissing counterclaims is subject to varying degrees of strength. The following represents unqualified [Qualify: no] dismissal: 'Alternatively, problems with validity ... can also be dismissed' (Text 2). On the other hand, the authors can tacitly acknowledge some doubt, as the following very hedged dismissal attests: [emphasis added] '... *we are relatively confident* that the differences ... cannot be accounted for by a control group that exhibits unusually low levels of psychiatric symptoms' (Text 8). Figures 4.11 and 4.12 depict the realization rules of this move in greater detail.

In sum, Moves B and D reiterate tensions that we have alluded to in earlier chapters. Generic structures either evolved from or are shaped by interpersonal needs. Within particular generic structures, we see ongoing conflicts between the scientist as neutral observer and as emotionally involved participant, and between the author as narrator of the tale and as protagonist.

Move E: state implications

As is true of 'ward off counterclaims', Move E, 'state implications', especially recommend future research, has become a prototypical genre structure, i.e. a norm usually observed. However, at least one previous author is recorded as protesting against such a move : 'Because [the study of motivation] is a high and

Figure 4.9 A partial system network for features of Move D, 'raise potential counterclaims'

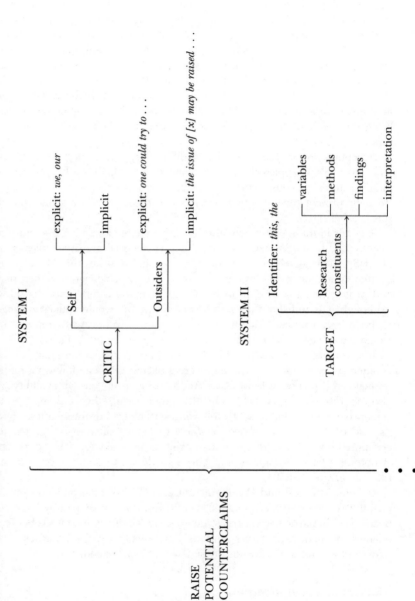

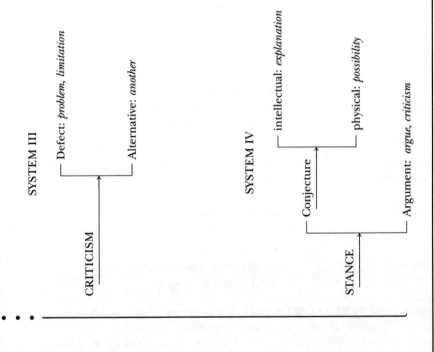

The items in italics are examples of realizations.

Figure 4.10 Realization rules for 'raise potential counterclaims'

FEATURE	REALIZATION
Critic	
Self:	
explicit	reference to authors: *we, our*
implicit	no person realized
Outsiders	
explicit	*one*
implicit	agent deletion in passive construction
Target	
	reference to the present research:
	identifier + constituent: *the findings*
Criticism	
Defect	attribute of target = context
	dependent: *these contradictory results*
Alternative	propose alternative explanation:
	another potential explanation [*is*]
Stance	
Conjecture	epistemic modality, e.g.
intellectual	*explanation*
	modal operator: *may, might*
physical	adjective: *possible*
	noun: *possibility*
	adverb: *perhaps*
Argument	verbal group: *make the case*
	nominal group: *argument*

Examples: [ALTERNATIVE CLAIM] 'One could try to make the case that Jennings is simply more facially expressive' (Text 7).

[DEFECT] 'There are several possible explanations for the poorer performance of [x variables] in explaining violent victimization. First, . . . our aggregate measure . . . may have suppressed the impact of [x] variables' (Text 2).

---

hazardous undertaking, I wish fewer people would meddle with it' (Montaigne, 1580: 126, cited in Bem, 1987).

In the contemporary world, this move may recommend future research, as in 'Further studies of other populations must therefore be performed to test the generalizability of these findings' (Text 10). Alternatively, or additionally, this

Figure 4.11   A partial system network for features for 'respond to potential counterclaims'

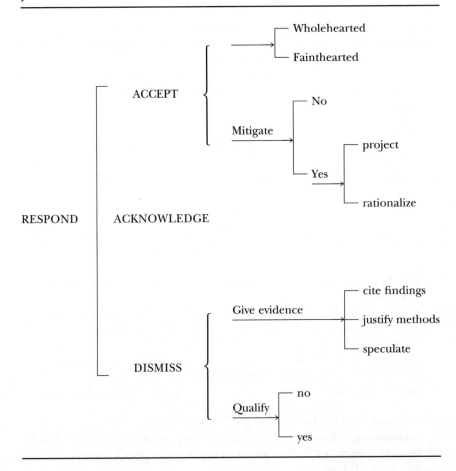

move may include practical applications to society (human behaviour) as: 'Our findings suggest that although male and female cocaine abusers are similar in many respects, differences can exist that would have ramifications for treatment' (Text 10).

Hence, four alternatives are open to authors:

1. to suggest no implications
2. to suggest implications for human behaviour only
3. to suggest implications for research and human behaviour
4. to suggest implications for research only.

The fourth option was the most frequently chosen, with five texts recommending only one avenue for future research, while three recommended several.

Figure 4.12 Realization rules for 'respond to potential counterclaims'

FEATURE	REALIZATION
Accept	identify self as source of problem
Wholehearted	defect = attribute of self (person or work): *our failure*
Fainthearted	defect = attribute of the present research product: *limitation of this study*
Mitigate	
project	blame external factors: defect = attribute of external factors
rationalize	trivialize defect
Acknowledge	plead lack of evidence for defect
Dismiss	
qualify: yes	insert hedge, e.g. attribution
no	no hedge

Examples:

1. **Wholehearted:** 'Thus the lack of [X] . . . may be due to our failure to evaluate how . . .' (Text 1).
2. **Fainthearted:** 'One limitation of this study is the fact that it took place at a single institution . . .' (Text 10). [RAISE POTENTIAL COUNTERCLAIM AND RESPOND CONFLATED]
3. **Mitigate: project:** 'These contradictory results may be due to the limited generalizability of sleep laboratory studies or to . . .' (Text 3).
4. **Mitigate: rationalize:** 'Although it is unlikely that withdrawal symptoms would influence long-term abstinence, a prospective study of [X] . . . would have been a much better test than the present study.' (Text 3).
5. **Acknowledge:** 'There is no way to rule out this possibility definitively' (Text 7).
6. **Dismiss: qualify: yes:** ' . . . we are relatively confident [that x is not a problem]' (Text 8).
7. **Dismiss: qualify: no:** ' . . . problems with validity can also be dismissed' (Text 2).

One might expect that a claim of relevance for human behaviour in Move 1 (see Chapter 3) would lead to a similar emphasis in the same authors' implications. However, when we compare the orientation in claiming relevance (Move 1) and in stating implications (Move E), we discover that not all orientations for human behaviour predict that a similar orientation will be found in Move E. However, implications for human behaviour in Move E are suggested only when such relevance has already been claimed in Move 1. There are logical reasons for the failure of symmetry; for one, implications for human behaviour cannot be suggested if the results have been contrary to the hypothesis. Secondly, an emphasis on research is needed to close any gaps which may have been opened in the previous *ward off* move.

The four alternatives in stating implications listed above reflect varying degrees of self-confidence. Implications for human behaviour express confidence that the research is 'correct' and has immediate application. The most dramatic example is the following text, which implies that the smiles of television newscasters can directly affect spectators' voting behaviour (underlining added to show reference to authors' own work):

> [A recent analysis by N ... suggested that] television news may help to define the standards by which presidents are evaluated ... Not only might the success of a particular program be so influenced, the selection of the president by the electorate may itself be influenced by which candidate the newscasters smile upon. (Text 7)

Making no recommendations for further research, the alternative adopted in three texts, suggests that the work is complete. 'Recommend further research', the most cautious alternative, can be adopted even when the authors have admitted no possible flaws in the research. It indicates that the present research can be expanded or even improved upon, laying the groundwork for future studies.

Also interesting is the disparity between rhetorical functions and lexicogrammatical realizations. Firstly, while these four rhetorical options represent a continuum of uncertainty about the strength of one's results, the lexicogrammatical realizations do not represent a continuum of uncertainty. In fact, most instances do not select uncertainty, e.g. 'Further studies on tobacco withdrawal will help determine . . .' (Text 3). Secondly, while the rhetorical function is to recommend, recommendations are not usually realized by a modal of obligation (such as 'should, ought to').

Among the five moves as a whole, the following pattern of modality emerges. 'Uncertainty' is the unmarked form in 'offer interpretation' (Move C) ('Perhaps the reason why children ... tended to receive ... was that they had established a history of . . .' Text 6), the common form in 'ward off counterclaims' (Move D) ('While the issue of [X] may be raised . . .' Text 5) and the marked form in 'state implications' (Move E) ('. . . longer-term investigations may be essential for a full appreciation of the impact . . .' Text 8).

Distribution of moves

In the sections 'The key moves' (p. 63) and 'How are moves realized in texts?' (p. 67) we provided definitions and realization criteria for the head act of each move. These specifications are necessary so that comparisons of moves across texts and across fields can be made. A further necessary step is to find out whether all texts of a genre share all moves. Table 4.2 indicates the distribution of moves in Discussion sections, by texts, and demonstrates that all the typical moves are not shared by all the texts. However, each text had one of (i) 'offer an interpretation' or (ii) 'ward off potential counterclaims'. A selection of one

Table 4.2 Distribution of 'moves' in Discussion section, by text

Move	Text number											
	1	2	3	4	5	6	7	8	9	10	11	12
Accomplish	✓	–	✓	✓	✓	✓	✓	✓	✓	✓	✓	✓
Evaluate	–	✓	✓	–	✓	✓	✓	✓	✓	✓	✓	✓
Interpret	–	✓	✓	✓	–	✓	✓	–	✓	✓	✓	✓
Ward off	✓	✓	✓	–	✓	✓	✓	✓	✓	✓	–	✓
Implications	✓	✓	✓	✓	✓	✓	✓	✓	✓	✓	–	–

alternative, then, would be the minimal obligatory structure for creating a Discussion section. Text 11, for instance, realizes only three of the five typical functions but it would be difficult to regard this or any of these texts as 'deficient' since all have been published in socially valued research journals.

As we have seen (Chapter 1), the traditional definition of genre, postulated by Hasan (Halliday and Hasan, 1985) is in terms of a minimum set of obligatory elements. The view we prefer, however, expounded by Martin (1992) and Ventola (1987, 1989), is that texts of a given genre exhibit prototypical structures, i.e. one can only say that membership of the texts in the same genre is established by the fact that they select their structures from a common repertoire and that there is a highly predictable sequence of structures.

But this still leaves unanswered the question of why different elements are found in different texts. To answer, we offer our view that a generic structure is not a metal mould into which text is 'poured' but rather one which interacts with the text, the two influencing each other. At the outset, certain elements of the context/situation (e.g. whether the results of the research were satisfactory to the authors) constrain the choice of a structure. As these choices are made, they constrain subsequent choices of structures. For example, 'offer interpretation' may not be realized because an extensive explanation for the hypothesis has been offered in the Introduction. The flowchart in Figure 4.13 (adopted from flowcharts of service encounters developed by Ventola, 1987) indicates the kinds of considerations that are presumed to affect the non-obligatory choices. We have limited these considerations to those that can be found in the text. Undoubtedly, much of the motivation for realizing specific moves lies outside of the text, for instance the decision to evaluate congruence may depend upon the existence of similar research that has to be acknowledged. Likewise, whether to state implications may rest upon constraints of time and space. This diagram symbolizes the first stage of the process the creator of text goes through; instead of filling a preconceived list of moves, decisions are made at each step (except that a choice of Move C or D must be made). At each move juncture, there is also a range of options, which we have tried to depict in the system networks. For instance, if the choice to realize 'ward off counterclaims' is made, the author must decide between projecting the criticism or identifying with it, and then between accepting the criticism or dismissing it. In this way, interpersonal needs mesh with the socially prescribed genre structure.

Extent of moves

We have seen that all Discussion texts in our corpus do not share all moves. A related issue is how far the selected genre structures can be stretched or contracted by the authors. Analysis of the first eight texts shows that even when the same rhetorical function is chosen, each text differs in the amount of attention allocated to it. The emphasis is shown in the proportion of clauses devoted to each move. While the major part of three of five texts that realize 'interpret' is devoted to this move, the major part of two, and almost one-half of a third text among eight, is expended on 'ward off counterclaims'. While 'implications' play the major role in two texts, they play a relatively minor role in the other six texts. These findings establish that the genre structure for research texts does not include an obligatory hierarchy for the amount of text which should be devoted to each move, a conclusion we found also obtained in the case of Introduction sections (Chapter 3).

Sequence of moves

We have described the prototypical moves for Discussion sections, the amount of text devoted to these moves, and possible variations in the selection of moves realized in a given text. We now turn to the issue of the prototypical sequencing of moves. That is, part of the realization of a social process, such as communicating to one's colleagues in a learned article, is through the order in which communicative structures occur. The primary choice in sequencing is whether moves are reiterated (cyclical patterning) or whether all moves of a given type, e.g. findings, are consolidated (composite form).

A common feature of Discussion sections in physical science research texts, according to Swales' (1990) survey of five relevant investigations, is the cyclic nature of the moves; each cycle consists of one result and other 'moves' related to that result. The cyclical nature of 'moves' was corroborated by Dubois (1997) for articles in biomedical journals. A composite form of discussion seems to be rare. However, the social science texts in the present study display much more variation in organization, allowing for both forms even within the same journal. This difference may be due to the difference in methods between our study and previous studies. Unlike previous studies, we have distinguished between ranks of generic elements – acts and moves. In addition, we have tried to characterize moves consistently by semantic criteria. Using these methods, we found that the texts in our corpus reflect three types of organization:

a. more than one discussion section (three texts)
   When more than one experiment was done, the results of each experiment

Figure 4.13 Flowchart representation of Discussion texts

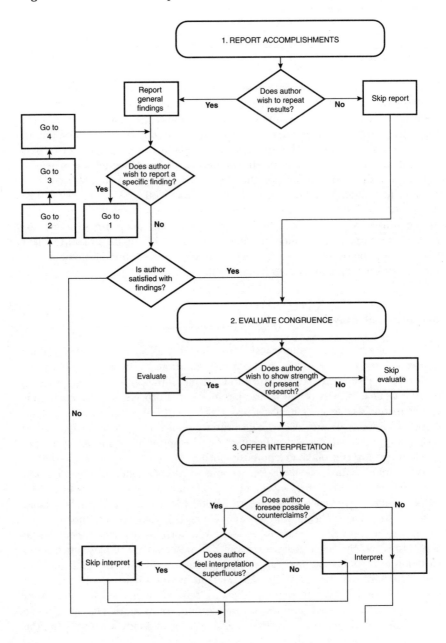

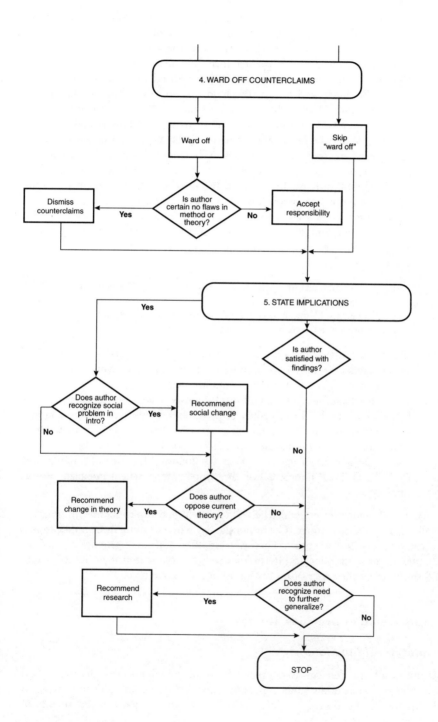

are found in individual discussion sections. Each individual discussion section consists of a cycle, with a minimum of two moves. The final, general discussion summarizes all the experiments.

b. single discussion section in cyclical form (two texts) ·

Two Discussion sections contain cycles realized by 'report accomplishments' (Findings) and any of the following moves: 'evaluate', 'interpret' and 'ward off'. One might assume that the 'cyclical' pattern was chosen because there was more than one result to report. This is not the case, however. While 11 out of the 12 texts report more than one result, only three texts are organized in cycles. When cycles occur, the organizing element is not a 'statement of results', in contrast to Hopkins and Dudley-Evans' (1988) findings. In one text, the head is a 'statement of phenomenon' with previous and present research findings and hypotheses as supporting acts. A second text is organized around social problems, with each cycle containing (1) a statement of a social problem that needed to be solved, (2) a research response to the problem and (3) results, as in the following example:

> In view of the fact that children's comfort and involvement in the school environment may be a necessary prerequisite for their educational progress [1 – social problem], it was also of interest to identify factors that . . . [2 – research response]. Analyses revealed that . . . [3 – results]. (Text 6)

If this pattern is found on a larger scale, it might underscore the need of social science to justify itself more in terms of its relevance to human behaviour than to novel empirical findings *per se*.

c. single discussion section with all results consolidated (seven texts), as in the following example: 'In this study of privately hospitalized cocaine abusers, we found many similarities as well as several differences between the sexes. Our data revealed that the women we studied generally began using cocaine at a younger age . . .' (Text 10) (followed by a list of findings and then the authors' interpretation and implications, which integrate all the findings).

As for sequence, in general when a 'report of accomplishments' (findings) is realized, it is the first move. Correspondingly, when 'statement of implications' is realized, it is the last move. The ordering of 'evaluate congruence', 'ward off counterclaims' and 'offer an interpretation' is flexible within these limits. Table 4.3 summarizes the order of moves found in the twelve texts.

Comparison to previous studies

Prototypical functions

At this point, it is relevant to compare the results obtained through our method with the results in other studies. In other words, can we find any similarities in the rhetorical functions in social science and physical science texts, in spite of

Table 4.3 Order of 'moves' by text

Text	Order of 'Moves'						
1. //R		W				IMP	//
2. //	E	W	O			IMP	//
‡3. //R	/ R and E,	O, or	$W/^{*}_{+}$			IMP	//
‡4. //R		O				IMP	//
5. # //R/	/R W/	/R/	/R	W		IMP	//
expt.:1	2	3	general discussion				
6. //R	/ R and E,	O, or	$W/^{*}_{+}$			IMP	//
7. # //	/ R W E/	/R/	R	O		IMP	//
expt.:	1	2	general discussion				
8. //R	W					IMP	//
9. //R	E	O	W			IMP	//
10. //R		O	W			IMP	//
11. //R O	/R E O/$^{*}_{+}$		R	O			//
12. # //	/ O R E W/	/R O/	W				//
expt.:	1	2	general discussion				

Key

//	= boundary of all discussion sections
/	= boundary of cycle
#	= includes individual discussion after each experiment and General Discussion sections
*	= order of the moves varies
+	= recursion
‡	= Result Section and Discussion are combined as 'Comment'
R	= report accomplishments
E	= evaluate congruence
W	= ward off counterclaims
O	= offer interpretations
IMP	= state implications
expt.	= experiment

the difference in methods of analysis? The comparison of the present results with those of previous classifications must also consider the differences in subgenres (proceedings of an international conference and MSc dissertations in Hopkins and Dudley-Evans [1988] compared to journal articles in the present study). Added to this are differences in field. Below we present a brief move from one text in our corpus. We apply the moves that seem to be representative of the discussion-analyses (see summary in Swales, 1990), most prominently by

Hopkins and Dudley-Evans (1988). This classification was later adapted by others, e.g. Holmes (1997), to the Discussion section of sociology, political science and history texts. Our judgements as to how to label acts in accordance with previous classifications were necessarily subjective, since no semantic criteria had been provided. In the following text, the labels of Hopkins and Dudley-Evans (1988) are underlined; the corresponding labels of the present study are in boldface, in square brackets.

[MOVE D – WARD OFF COUNTERCLAIMS]

EXPLANATION OF UNSATISFACTORY RESULT – [**A. raise potential counterclaim**] 'While the issue of procedural sensitivity may be raised in the context of these negative findings,
REFERENCE TO PREVIOUS RESEARCH – [**B. respond**] [**1. evaluate congruence**] the visual fixation paradigms used in this series of studies have been shown in the past to be sensitive to infants' selective attentional responses to auditory stimuli [references].
STATEMENT OF RESULT – [**2. report finding**] Furthermore, infants' attention to stimuli in Experiment 1 was sufficient to allow readily observable discrimination.
DEDUCTION OR HYPOTHESIS – [**offer conclusion**] If the salience of a stimulus parameter is observable only within certain procedural constraints . . . the parameter cannot be considered to be a powerful one. The consistency of the results across the two techniques and three different stimuli employed in these studies suggests this to be the case.
? – [**comment**] Given the pervasiveness of exaggerated intonation or modulation patterns in adult-to-infant speech, these negative results become all the more interesting' (Text 5).

In the proposed method, judgements are made according to communicative purpose; then the segments are labelled. This is in contrast to applying labels established in previous studies. Some of the main differences in the two approaches become apparent. First, the Hopkins and Dudley-Evans (1988) classification is based on what we have defined as acts, and therefore does not indicate any structure at a higher level of generalization; as presently labelled, the individual acts are not included in a function at a higher rank. For instance, what is the extent of 'explanation of unsatisfactory result'? In addition, the difference between 'statement of results' as a move and as an act in support of another move is not established.

Second, the difference is not clear in the previous approach between deduction and hypothesis. Third, reference to previous research is categorized according to purpose in our system. Fourth, some acts such as *comment* do not appear in previous corpora except for biomedical texts (Dubois, 1997).

Table 4.4 compares move classification of Discussion sections in the present study and in others we have cited. Out of the 21 rhetorical functions determined by other authors, only three – *results*, *hypothesis* and *recommendation* – are common to the majority of the present texts and fit our definition of a move (an obligatory

Table 4.4 Comparison of 'moves' in Discussion sections as determined by five previous studies and the present study

Move	Author					
	B	H	P	D	RH	LFY
1. Introduction	✓	–	–	–	–	–
Background information	–	✓	✓	–	✓	–
Common knowledge	–	–	–	r	–	–
2. Summarizing results	✓	✓	✓	r	✓	✓
3. Conclusions, deduction	✓	✓	✓	r	–	act
4. What results suggest	✓	–	–	–	–	–
5. Further questions	✓	–	–	–	–	–
6. Possible answers to future questions	✓	–	–	–	–	–
7. (Un)expected outcome*	–	✓	✓	–	✓	–
8. Reference to previous research	✓	✓	–	r	✓	–
9. Explain unsatisfactory result	–	✓	–	–	✓	–
10. Exemplification*	–	✓	–	–	–	–
11. Hypothesis*	–	✓	✓	r	–	✓
12. Recommendation*	–	✓	✓	–	✓	✓
13. Justification*	–	✓	✓	–	–	act
14. Observation	–	–	✓	–	–	–
15. Comparison	–	–	✓	–	–	–
16. Validation	–	–	✓	–	–	–
17. Metatext	–	–	–	r	–	act
18. Explanation	–	–	✓	–	–	–
19. Methodology	–	–	–	r	–	act
20. Comment*	–	–	–	r	–	act
21. Developments*	–	–	–	–	✓	–

Key
B   = Belanger, neuroscience, 1982, cited in Dubois, 1997
H   = Hopkins and Dudley-Evans, biology and agriculture, 1988
P   = Peng, chemical engineering, 1987, cited in Dubois, 1997
D   = Dubois, biomedicine, 1997
RH = Holmes, social science and history, 1997
LFY = The present study
✓   = considered a 'move'
r   = considered a 'rhetorical function'

* **Definitions**
 7.   = remarks on whether the result is expected or not
10.   = an example to support the author's explanation.
11.   = a more general claim arising from the experimental results
12.   = suggestions for future work
13.   = justification of recommendations for future research
20.   = author's evaluation or judgement
21.   = outlining parallel or subsequent developments

act with slots for optional acts). The previous studies cited all found 'summarizing results' as the obligatory element in Discussion sections, whereas this element is missing in one social science text. (See Accomplish, Table 4.2.) Five functions considered as moves by one or more previous authors (*conclusions, justification, metatext, methodology* and *comment*) appear infrequently in our texts and then only as acts within larger moves. On the other hand, previous literature does not recognize 'evaluate congruence' and 'ward off counterclaims' as moves.[2] However, later, Dudley-Evans (1994) introduced the move 'limitation', in which the writers introduce one or more caveats about their findings, methodology or claims. This move may overlap with some of the features of *ward off counterclaims*.

Of the three major structures in common (*results, hypothesis* and *recommendation*), only *hypothesis* was defined as the selection of uncertainty (Dubois, 1997; Hopkins and Dudley-Evans, 1988; Dudley-Evans, 1994). While selection for uncertainty, specifically the modal 'may' or the lexical verb 'suggest', characterizes the overwhelming majority of instances of the act 'offer hypothesis' in the present study, this act may also be realized by selecting neutral modality as in 'Another mechanism to account for tobacco withdrawal is that withdrawal symptoms represent a simple behavioural reaction . . .' (Text 3). Even a modal of certainty can be chosen as in 'The causal mechanism for this explanation must involve the subtle operation of . . .' (Text 7). These latter two types of realizations have not been reported in analyses of physical science texts.

In sum, the different sets of texts were analysed by different methods, with the result that the present study distinguishes between macro (moves) and micro (acts) functions. The present study recognizes five macro functions (three of which are exemplified in Text 5 at the beginning of this chapter), while previous studies combined recognize 21 functions, of units of unspecified rank. Unfortunately, we cannot know if all these differences are due to FIELD (social science as against physical sciences) or to the different methods in the two sets of analyses.

Focus on two acts

Although the macro units in this study of social science texts are not comparable to those in previous studies of physical sciences, as we have said above, it would still be interesting to know if any units at a lower rank are comparable. We have chosen to analyse the two functions common to past studies and the present study for which definitions were provided by past studies: *offering comments* and *stating conclusions*.

In three previous studies, *stating conclusions or deductions* is considered a move, while *comment* is recognized only by Dubois (1997), who does not distinguish between moves and acts but considers both 'rhetorical functions' (see Table 4.4). It is not clear if the reason for this disparity is that 'comments' are specific to the field of biomedicine, which she studied, or that analysts of Discussion sections in other fields overlooked this category.

In the method of classification adopted for this study, these two functions are considered acts, which are a component of moves.

Stating comments

It can be argued that every rhetorical act in a text is, in some sense, a comment by the author, since the decision to include an act entails an assessment of its importance. However, for purposes of comparison, the following working definition was adopted. To begin with, a comment overtly expresses a writer's evaluation or judgement (Dubois, 1997). In addition, from our perspective, a comment theoretically can fill a slot in any move and can be omitted without impinging on the intelligibility of the move. (See definition of move, Chapter 2.) A further criterion is that we will consider as *comments* only assertions which do not realize another act. Using this definition, we found twenty instantiations of comments, comprising 24 clauses, or two per cent of the total number of clauses in twelve texts. In both our study and that of Dubois (1997), common comments were *interesting* and *important*. Comments perform the following functions:

1. highlighting one of a series of results or explanations as 'special'
2. directing the reader in drawing appropriate conclusions
3. expressing satisfaction with one's own research
4. pointing out a disparity between expectations and reality. Type (4) is not to be confused with 'evaluate congruence', which is identified by the realization criteria in Figure 4.8. Comments that imply the result was unexpected were not marked by signals such as 'surprising'. Instead of admitting outright surprise, which might jeopardize their status as neutral observers, the authors present such results rather opaquely, e.g. 'Although the results fit the general multidimensional expectations quite nicely, they were more complex than anticipated' (Text 12). Note other examples in Table 4.5.
5. expressing lack of understanding/skepticism.

These types of comments show that editorializing on scientific claims is permitted by the genre. Although relatively few in number, they form still another thread in the prominent interpersonal strand in scientific texts. Dubois (1997) is equally surprised that comments occur as frequently as they do 'since in the quest for absolute objectivity, the *normative scientist* . . . would be presumed to refrain from expressing opinion, letting the facts speak for themselves' (p. 20).

Stating conclusions

Four previous studies include a category of moves labelled 'conclusion' or 'deduction' although three studies do not provide definitions of either.[3] (See Table 4.4.) But Dubois (1997: 11) differentiates 'conclusion' from 'hypothesis' as follows (italics are in the original):

Conclusions were identified notionally by their place at the end (less often, at the beginning) of a chain of reasoning, [OR] by the presence of a conjunctive adverbial

Table 4.5 Comments in Discussion sections, by function

Text Number

Highlighting one or more results or explanations as special
3. This possibility is interesting because . . .
4. Of considerable interest in this respect is . . .
7. . . . we consider this explanation to be the most plausible one.
7. Although direct causation . . . is more parsimonious and to us more plausible than indirect, independent causation [there is no way to rule out this possibility definitively].
9. Of special interest is the fact that . . .
9. Most noteworthy are the differential roles . . .
11. Most interestingly, . . . we found . . .

Directing the reader in drawing appropriate conclusions
4. This linkage should not be overlooked or disdained merely because of the low level of the relationship.
4. The failure to differentiate the diagnostic groups with respect to [x] should not be interpreted as indicating that . . .
5. It does not seem reasonable, therefore, to attribute the salience of motherese to young infants to this parameter alone.
6. It should be noted, however, that little or no relation was found.
7. It is important to note that these biases . . . were not merely part of a systematic pattern.
8. Although these data must be interpreted cautiously . . .
12. The similarity between the patterns observed here and the various dimensional schemes is important in demonstrating that . . .
12. The more important point is that M's (1987) judgement . . . differs importantly from that of R (1984).

Expressing satisfaction with one's own research
8. . . . we are relatively confident that [the differences between the . . . groups cannot be accounted for by . . .]
8. . . . we are encouraged by the viability and meaningfulness of the results.

Pointing out a disparity between expectations and reality
5. [Given the pervasiveness of exaggerated intonation of modulation patterns in adult-to infant speech,] these negative results become all the more interesting.
8. Interestingly, there were no differences between [x] and controls on some variables.
12. Although the results fit the general multidimensional expectations quite nicely, they were more complex than anticipated.
12. This array of additional effects of expressions seems at first glance to be chaotic and unpredictable. In fact, it was not predicted [but is very consistent with many . . . models . . .]

Expressing lack of understanding/skepticism
7. If true, this explanation would hold great theoretical interest.
12. [Study 2] Why he reached this conclusion is somewhat unclear . . .

* Material in brackets added to give context.

such as *thus* or *therefore* and if there was a modal verb, by the presence of *must* or *have to*, which indicate certainty.

(We added [OR] because her examples indicate that she considered either criterion as sufficient.) Hypotheses, on the other hand, always include 'the presence of common forms of modality indicating various degrees of uncertainty' (p. 11). Thus, in Dubois' system, the functions of offering 'conclusions' and 'hypothesis' are not defined by the author's intent but by the lexicogrammatical realizations (which differs from our approach). However, for the purpose of this comparison, we defined 'conclusions' by lexicogrammatical criteria. We selected all assertions in Discussion sections which contain a lexical marker of conclusion, namely:

1. conjunctive adverbs of conclusion, as sentence modifiers only: *thus, therefore, hence, consequently.*
2. expressions of conviction: *clearly, it is clear, undoubtedly; [x] cannot be*
3. lexemes of *conclude*

Based on these criteria, we found that:

1. the most common signal of 'conclusion' is 'Thus'
2. the lexeme 'conclude' with the present authors as agents or source appears only three times in the Discussion texts. In two of these instances, the word *conclusion* is a second reference in a reference chain while the initial lexical item is actually *hypothesis*. Thus, the hypotheses became more certain at second mention. Conclusions do appear, however, as first item in the reference chain, when the source is another author, e.g. 'Past researchers have concluded . . .' (Text 8), which raises an interesting question about the original (cited) literature: Did the authors use a weaker verb than 'conclude' such as 'hypothesize' when referring to their own acts? This is a question we have not attempted to answer at present but it warrants future study.
3. lexically signalled conclusions comprised only 72 clauses or five per cent of the 1350 clauses in the Discussion section in the present corpus of SSR texts compared to eight per cent of the independent clauses in biomedical texts (Dubois, 1997). The low number of conclusion-acts does not mean that social scientists refrain from conclusions; it is equally plausible that they tend not to signal conclusions lexically, e.g. 'These results demonstrate that facial feedback effects are not unidimensional' (Text 12).

    When *conclusion* is not encoded in the linguistic realizations, the outside reader cannot know if an assertion such as the above is a report of an observable fact (a result) or a product of reasoning. Hence, any analysis of 'conclusions' would have to be restricted to those specifically marked by the author.
4. when authors do use markers of conclusion (including markers of conviction) they co-occur with a 'hedge' in 50 per cent of the sentences, i.e. of the 44 sentences which select a structure of conclusion or conviction, 22 sentences simultaneously select a structure of uncertainty, including lexical

verbs such as 'seems', e.g. 'Thus, it seems clear that . . .' (Text 7).

In such assertions, conviction is 'neutralized' logically by uncertainty. Whether the reader interprets this kind of sentence as 'neutral' is another subject that should be pursued. When an act of conclusion does not select for uncertainty within the sentence, it is often followed by a sentence realizing 'uncertainty', which serves the same function: to weaken the conclusion.

5. of the 44 sentences of conclusions, 22 do not hedge their claims within the sentence, presenting what Myers (1989) alludes to as the 'bald-on-record strategy'. But based on the analysis outlined in Table 4.6, these unmitigated conclusions are not all claims which represent an addition to the ongoing discussion of the particular phenomena under study; therefore, they do not represent a challenge to the scientific community. Four of the examples realize the act 'accept responsibility' (for deficiencies in the research). Other statements report previous authors' 'conclusions', recommend future research, evaluate the congruence of present research, or report findings.

Thus, unmitigated conclusions can be mapped onto various rhetorical functions and the majority of unmitigated conclusions do not herald new explanations for phenomena. Based on their content, only seven sentences (F, in Table 4.6) can be regarded as presenting a new knowledge claim. These seven instances of new knowledge claims are concentrated in only four texts which means they are posited by only four sets of authors.

How can we explain the fact that most conclusions are hedged by a feature of 'uncertainty'? One possibility is that hedging of new claims can be regarded as a reflection of modesty or real uncertainty as to whether their claims are accurate. However, Myers (1989: 3) argues that hedging represents one of the '. . . rational strategies for dealing with the social interactions involved in publishing an article'. If we accept the theory that a new claim is, in some sense, an effrontery to the audience because it disturbs the status quo and, as we have indicated in our discussion on 'gaps', often seeks to redress a wrong committed by a previous researcher, a politeness strategy is called for. It would seem necessary to frame one's claims as tentative until accepted by the entire discourse community for whom the findings are relevant.

Although the present corpus is composed of social science texts, and Myers' corpus was drawn from molecular biology, our findings that most conclusions are hedged, and that only a minority of the non-hedged involve claims of new knowledge, support Myers' (1989: 13) contention that 'the hedging of claims is so common that a sentence that looks like a claim but has no hedging is probably not a statement of new knowledge'. Myers argues that we find the 'bald-on-record' strategy (no hedging) when 'the imposition on the reader is so small it can be ignored or where the demands for efficiency are so great that they override the demands of politeness'. The non-hedged conclusions found in this corpus, especially the acts of self-criticism, do not represent an imposition upon the status quo.

Table 4.6 Sentences in Discussion sections that signal for 'conclusion' and do not select for 'uncertainty' within the sentence, by category

Extra text necessary to supply context is enclosed in square brackets.

A CONCLUSIONS ABOUT THE METHODS USED:

1. **Undoubtedly**, referential comparisons are much more constrained by local settings and persons' comparisons of fairness must reside primarily within the [x]. (Text 1)

2. **Thus**, the vignette approach used here places too great an emphasis on . . . (Text 1)

3. Our analysis of persons' justice sentiments was **therefore** made outside of the local comparative context. (Text 1)

4. **Consequently**, the potential for subtle influences is always present. (Text 12)

B REPORT OF PREVIOUS AUTHORS' 'CONCLUSIONS':

5. Past researchers concerned with [x] have **concluded** that . . . (Text 8)

6. As N, N, & N have **concluded** . . . (Text 8)

C RECOMMENDATION FOR FUTURE RESEARCH:

7. **Consequently**, whether social trends that improve the quality of life for some groups . . . remains a question for further research. (Text 2)

8. These **conclusions** are contingent on . . . (Text 9)

9. Further studies of other populations must **therefore** be performed to test the generalizability of these findings. (Text 10)

D EVALUATION OF CONGRUENCE OF PRESENT RESEARCH

10. **Thus**, these results are consistent with past literature.

E REPORT OF FINDINGS OR CONCLUSIONS OF FACT, NOT INTERPRETATIONS:

11. **Thus**, during abstinence the subjects were as distressed as the average psychiatric outpatient. (Text 3)

12. **Consequently**, . . . children were faced with the task of forming new relationships and gaining acceptance in a new peer group. (Text 6)

13. Whereas a similar **conclusion** can be drawn about the relation between the range of prior peer contexts and children's nurse requests in kindergarten, the same cannot be said about classroom anxiety and absences. (Text 6)

14. We can at least **conclude** that, by age 4, the two groups are approximately equivalent in IQ [after giving boys and girls Picture Vocabulary test]. (Text 11)

15. **Thus**, the secondary emotions produced by the expressions were those that were nearest . . . (Text 12)

Table 4.6 Sentences in Discussion sections that signal for 'conclusion' and do not select for 'uncertainty' within the sentence, by category (*cont.*)

F NEW KNOWLEDGE CLAIMS

16. The causal mechanism for this explanation **must** involve the subtle operations of emotional associative cues, which dictated choice of news program despite the lack of content bias. (Text 7)

17. **Clearly**, an explanation in terms of context effect cannot account for the differences . . . (Text 8)

18. **Thus**, the life stress process leading to physical symptoms is more significantly conditioned by [x]. (Text 9)

19. Nonetheless, it is **quite clear** that social resources play a dominating role . . . (Text 9)*

20. **Thus**, no unidimensional factor could produce this pattern of results (Text 12).

21. **Thus**, for postures, as for facial expressions, the effects on experience reflect more than a single dimension of variation. (Text 12)

22. At the very least, however, **it is clear** that a moderate effect of facial feedback is not necessarily inconsistent with many theories . . . (Text 12).

---

* There is some difference of opinion as to whether 'quite' is a weakener or intensifier in this context.

Strengthening Myers' argument is his observation that when the new claim becomes part of the literature, it is then permissible to refer to it without any hedging, which explains why we find: '[Outside author] concludes' but not 'we conclude'.

Thus, the act of offering conclusions is realized rarely in SSR texts. When it is realized, conclusions involving new claims are tempered by hedging. While persuasion seems to be the driving force behind many of the rhetorical functions in these texts, persuasion gives way to reticence when authors express conclusions about their interpretations of findings.

Summary

As we have seen, Discussion sections are comprised of five prototypical moves:

 A. report accomplishments;
 B. evaluate congruence of findings to other criteria;
 C. offer interpretation;
 D. ward off counterclaims;
 E. state implications.

Our research shows that the only obligatory element is the inclusion of either Move C or D. Each text contains at least one obligatory move and two optional moves. In addition, Moves A and E, where realized, are the first and last moves, respectively, but the ordering of B, C and D is flexible within these fixed points.

Moves can be realized in composite or in cyclical form. If one considers only the last (general) discussion section, when discussions of all individual experiments are included, then the composite form is more typical. Authors can decide not only which of the prototypical moves to realize but also how much to highlight each move, i.e. the proportion of text to devote to each move.

We have provided a system for generating realizations of each move. Within the realization for Moves B, C, D and E, there are further variations in structures. The most interpersonal move is D ('ward off counterclaims') in which the authors project a potential counterclaim and respond by either accepting responsibility for a limitation in the present study or by dismissing the counterclaim. In Move E authors may state implications for human behaviour and/or for research but tend to do the latter. Moves C and D, both assertions about hypothetical conditions, are usually hedged, specifically by realizing the feature 'uncertainty' in various forms.

Two rhetorical functions, *stating comments* and *stating conclusions*, not considered moves according to our methods, were studied in order to compare these findings to previous findings. *Stating comments* was found to be a rare act but one that fulfilled clear-cut purposes. *Stating conclusions* represents only 5 per cent of the clauses in Discussion sections. We find that conclusions are not always signalled as conclusions; furthermore, acts marked as conclusions frequently co-occur with a structure of uncertainty, thereby neutralizing the definiteness of the conclusion. This failure to 'conclude' decisively may be a function of the need to dilute new claims so that impositions are not made upon the reader, another reflection of politeness strategies (Brown and Levinson, 1987).

In every sense, a scientific research text is an argument and theoretically only reporting results is necessary for establishing one's contribution to science. Moves 2–5 ('evaluate congruence of findings to other criteria', 'offer interpretation', 'ward off potential counterclaims', 'state implications') have mainly rhetorical functions in convincing the reader of the validity of the claims therein. The next step would be to understand how these particular moves developed and their place in establishing and reinforcing scientific claims. Furthermore, since not all moves are realized in every text, speculation is in order as to the kinds of factors that motivate particular moves, for instance, whether a majority or a minority view of the field is being posited or whether the authors are novices or more esteemed veteran members of the profession.

Notes

1. This wording of the definition is especially important since authors sometimes use lexical verbs of uncertainty such as 'suggest' or 'appear' to report findings (as well as interpretations), as in sentence (1) below. Thus, selecting 'modality' or, in particular,

uncertainty as a sufficient criterion for an interpretation would lead the reader astray. Evidence that the purpose of sentence (1) is to report a finding is found in sentence (2), which clearly shows the claim 'that the majority of children were not members . . .' is based on numerical data.

(1) 'Our data also suggests [sic] that the majority of children's classmates were not members of their preschool classrooms or non-school peer networks.'

(2) 'Children enrolled in the target kindergarten classrooms came from more than twelve preschools and the proportion of familiar peers in their kindergarten classrooms averaged seventeen per cent for males and sixteen per cent for females.' (Text 6)

Furthermore, we have defined the report of findings and interpretation on the basis of linguistic structures. However, one questions whether the phenomena being represented – a report of a finding and an interpretation – can be so clearly demarcated into two separate entities. For instance:

(3) 'The results of Study I can be summarized as follows.

(4) Subjects were able to detect differences in positivity of facial expressions of newscasters that occurred during reference to unequivocally positive or negative events.' (Text 7)

Sentence (4) qualifies as a report of findings on linguistic evidence: it immediately follows an initial boundary for 'results'; it discusses a fact which could be reducible to a statistical relation; past tense establishes (4) as a statement of fact rather than conjecture. However, this actually means the authors interpreted a certain score on this scale as 'detecting differences', and then decided how much statistical evidence would be necessary to generalize into 'Subjects were able to detect differences' (Text 7).

2. However, McKinley (1982, cited by Dubois, 1997) isolated a move she termed 'anticipating possible objections'.

3. Hopkins and Dudley-Evans (1988) offer the following definitions of these two acts: 'Deduction, in which the writer makes a claim about the generalisability of the particular results . . . Hypothesis, in which the writer makes a more general claim arising from his experimental results . . .'. Dudley-Evans (1994) later collapses these two categories into one, 'claim', in which the writers make a generalization arising from their results, which is their contribution to the ongoing research on the topic. He notes that claims tend to be hedged.

5 The tie that binds: lexical cohesion

Introduction

Having examined the ways in which rhetorical structure creates SSR texts, we can turn our attention to the role of word choices in the creation of these texts. Research texts, like all texts, are formed by different kinds of structures that relate constituents such as moves and acts to each other. As we have seen in preceding chapters, the rhetorical structure of moves creates the horizontal structuring in a text, with each move accounting for a segment of the text. However, there are also dependency structures that relate entities vertically. This chapter and Chapter 6 deal with such dependencies and the systems that lie behind them: lexical cohesion and reference respectively. At the micro level, the vertical discourse elements of lexical cohesion and reference are interwoven throughout the moves of a text to bind units into a unified text.

The first of these two resources on the vertical dimension, lexical cohesion, is defined by Halliday and Hasan (1976: 274) as the 'cohesive effect achieved by the selection of vocabulary'. To explain this notion fully, we must see lexical cohesion as one of the devices for linking parts of a text together. More generally, 'cohesion occurs where the interpretation of some element in the discourse is dependent on that of another. The one presupposes the other, in the sense that it cannot be effectively decoded except by recourse to it' (Halliday and Hasan, 1976: 4). For example, in the second sentence of this paragraph, 'this notion' is dependent on the sentence before it and can only be interpreted by knowing this earlier information. A link is thus established between the earlier information and the dependent item 'this notion'. If there are many links, then a chain is formed that contributes to the texture of the text.

Cohesion may be achieved by grammatical means such as proforms (e.g. pronouns) or ellipsis, or by lexical means. The lexical cohesive choices create the effect of unity with common meanings running through it. A preference for lexical rather than grammatical cohesion is shared by written texts, in contrast to oral texts, which rely heavily on grammatical systems. Scientific texts, in particular, use lexical cohesion to ensure continuity and to reduce ambiguity. Among the types of lexical cohesion, there is a preference for items that are more literal and unambiguous (connotative and univocal in terms of

Kinneavy, 1971). Thus, it is not surprising that repetition or paraphrasing are the resources that are favoured in scientific texts (de Beaugrande and Dressler, 1981).

When we consider lexical choices in a text, we have to explain why these particular words are selected. The concept of register describes the most significant source. This concept predicts that choices of vocabulary derive from a reservoir of options related to field (oriented to the social activity and task at hand), mode (related to the channel of communication), and tenor (related to the social relationships of the individuals communicating). Collectively, selections from this reservoir of meanings, lexical and other, create a particular register (Halliday, 1978; Martin, 1992). For example, in a conversation between a father and child playing with a wooden train, the field, reflecting the social processes, expresses itself in choices of verbs having to do with movement, nominal groups representing the objects being played with, and adjuncts of location. Similar lexical items could be found in related genres such as that of buying a toy. The different genres would be related by a common field instantiated by the lexical choices, but the genres themselves would relate to different social processes. On the other hand, a genre, such as primary school lessons, may have one basic macro structure reflecting the social process of teaching but have a variety of lexical sets associated with it (arithmetic, history or current events). The mode in the example of the father and son playing, above, is task oriented, which is reflected in the use of pronouns such as 'I' and 'you' and exophoric reference such as 'this car', which all depend on the common knowledge of the physical context of the interaction. There may also be elements of ellipsis in such an encounter, such as a one-word response to the command: 'Move the red train./ Okay.' The tenor selections tend to be interwoven throughout the phrase involving selections such as mood, modality and attitudinal elements, which reflect the ways in which the speakers control each other and express their wishes; for example, by structures such as 'want Daddy to . . .' or the father commanding the son to do something with the train, as in 'Put the train on the track again'.

In sum, the lexical selections, and especially lexical cohesion, reflect field, mode and tenor, the register of the texts, as well as the genre. The choice of lexis can thus be seen as being controlled by the higher level semantic categories of register and genre. (For the use of cohesion tied to these higher levels and to the difficulties of different kinds of speakers, see Fine [1994]).

Lexical cohesion and genre

Classification systems

Before specifically studying scientific texts at the micro level, in order to examine the ways in which lexical cohesion ties together units of a text, we have to devise a method for classifying the relationships between lexical items. Halliday and Hasan (1976) identified the following relationships between lexical items:

Reiteration:
(a) general word; e.g. thing: book
(b) repetition (including items with the same lexical root); e.g. book: book
(c) synonym; e.g. volume: book (and including hyponymy; e.g. rose: flower)
(d) near synonym; e.g. carpet: broadloom
(e) superordinate; e.g. flower: tulip

Collocation:
Based on mutual expectancy and proximity among items; e.g. bread: butter; pencil: paper

These categories with the exception of repetition are rather loose ones that depend on the subjective judgements of the listener or reader. For example, one objection is that no two lexical items are exact synonyms, as the following pair shows:

Faulkner wrote that book.
Faulkner wrote that volume.

The concept of a near synonym is even more difficult to define.

Martin (1992) points out some additional problems in the original Halliday and Hasan approach. For one, Halliday and Hasan do not present criteria to distinguish hyponymy and superordination. Furthermore, collocation depends on statistical relationships such that the occurrence of one lexical item predicts the distribution of other lexical items. Hasan (Halliday and Hasan, 1985) later dropped the category of collocation as an independent category, as well as superordination and general word, suggesting instead that collocates be identified on the basis of the other categories of lexical relationships. These revised categories, with examples, are:

Repetition – leave, leaving, left
Synonymy – leave, depart
Antonymy – leave, arrive
Hyponymy – travel, leave; rose, tulip (as co-hyponyms)
Meronymy – hand, finger (as co-meronyms)

Similar categories of lexical relations are offered by Martin (1992), who divides hyponymy into hyponymy and co-hyponymy and divides meronymy into meronymy and co-meronymy as follows:

Hyponymy – flower, tulip
Co-hyponymy – tulip, rose
Contrast – buy, sell
Synonymy – quick, fast
Repetition – pencil, pencils
Meronymy – house, window
Co-meronymy – window, door

Despite Martin's extensions and revisions, fuzzy categories remain problematic. A solution, however, can be found by forming system networks that specify progressively more delicate distinctions, reading from left to right through the network (as in Figure 5.1). Similarly, within a particular field such as gardening, taxonomies can be constructed to show the fine distinctions among categories of lexical items (as in Figure 5.2).

The categories of lexical cohesion can then be mapped onto the taxonomy of lexical distinctions for a specific field. For example, 'Babylon' and 'Golden' from the taxonomy of trees, can be seen as hyponyms of the category to their left; namely, willow. Similarly, 'amur' and 'Norway' share the features of tree: rounded: maple. Lexical relations can then be assigned to additional lexical items as they appear in a text on the basis of the features presented in the systems of lexical relations (see Martin, 1992, Chapter 5 and the systems presented there).

Lexical cohesion as a reflection of genre

With a method for classifying lexical cohesion, we can investigate how lexical cohesion interacts with genre. The questions are:

(1) Do texts of a single genre use 'the same cohesive building materials' (Ventola, 1987: 130)? If there are common patterns in the use of lexical cohesion, then this is some supporting evidence that the texts belong to the same genre. (In terms of metafunctional considerations, this is a textual matter.)

(2) What do the patterns of lexical cohesion reveal about the semiotic organization of the texts? Lexical cohesion may reflect the semantic levels of both genre and register (Ventola, 1987). For example, a discussion of money with the appropriate choices in vocabulary ('change', 'coins', 'notes') reflects a genre and also the specific move of purchase. But since money is common to many encounters in society, the lexical choices may reflect the field of discourse and so be an aspect of register. (Once again, in terms of metafunctional considerations, this is largely an ideational matter.)

(3) The orientation of the present study leads us to ask, 'Do the chains of lexical choices also reflect the interpersonal aspect of scientific writing?' This is an important question because the interpersonal needs of a writer also contribute to the construction of a text within a particular genre. In scientific writing, these interpersonal needs are the need to appear important or, in contrast, to appear modest. For example, a non-factive noun ('view') can be used to describe another author's ideas, whereas the more impressive 'theory' can be used to describe one's own ideas (Swales, 1987). Similarly, Bazerman (1984), who followed the revision of a scientific article, reports that the certainty of a claim (that is a key element of interpersonal interaction) was revised: 'fact' was weakened to 'observation'; a 'theory' was demoted to a 'hypothesis'; 'supposed' was strength-

Figure 5.1   Contrast systems in English

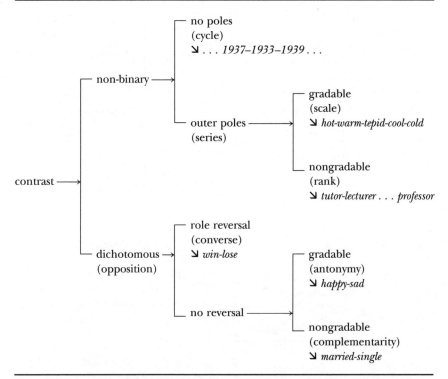

Adapted from Martin 1992: 304, used with permission of John Benjamins Publishing Co. The items in italics are examples of realizations.

ened to 'explained'. This fluctuation in the presentation of certainty indicates clearly the type of interpersonal considerations that are an integral part of scientific writing, and that genre choices may be fine-tuned in accordance with interpersonal needs.

Method of analysis

We followed three steps in the analysis of lexical cohesion.

(1) All the content words (more technically, words from open classes of lexical items) that appeared in the narrative strand of the Introduction and Discussion sections of Texts 1–8 were analysed. Because research articles were drawn from different disciplines in the social sciences, lexis dealing with the phenomena themselves and the particular variables were not analysed. High frequency lexical items in common usage (e.g. 'do',

Figure 5.2 Taxonomy of lexical items in trees

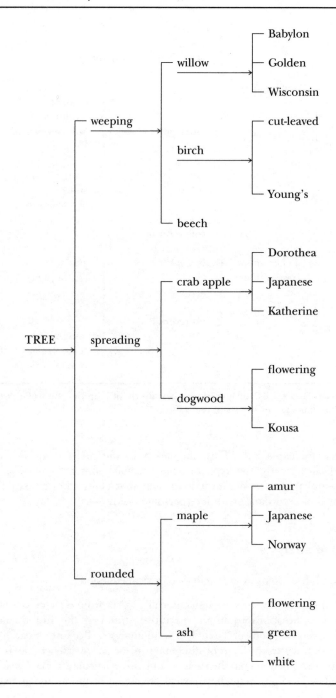

'years') were also excluded; however, there were very few such words in the texts. The analysis then focused only on the lexical items that create the narrative strand in the articles of this scientific register.

(2) The selected content words were then grouped into semantic categories, following Martin and Peters (1985). In this framework, for example, lexical items such as 'unclear', 'neglected', and 'question', which do not share a morpheme or a grammatical category (e.g., adjective, verb), are grouped together to form a lexical string since they share the semantic field of *problem* (see p. 73). A lexical string is composed of items in a category that appear in a sequence. The minimal length of a string for this study was three lexical items; furthermore, only semantic categories found in more than one of these texts were considered. This approach was designed to uncover the regularities in lexical patterning that contribute to the genre of the texts. This patterning helps both writers and readers of SSR texts to recognize that the text belongs to the given genre.

(3) Lexical cohesion was classified according to a system simplified from that of Martin as discussed above (p. 105). The following categories accounted for all the lexical ties found in the texts:

1. **repetition**
   a. *complete*: tokens in the tie are identical, e.g. 'theory', 'theory'
   b. *partial*: tokens in the tie share the same lexeme, e.g. 'theory', 'theoretical'
2. **replacement**
   c. *synonymy*: tokens in the tie are synonyms (entailing that they belong to the same grammatical category), e.g. 'population', 'inhabitants'. The term *synonym* refers to lexical items that share semantic features at a primary level of delicacy. (These features are displayed in Figure 5.3.) For example, 'hypothesis' and 'conclusion' share the basic features [product of reasoning: research register] but differ in the degree of firmness that the speaker is conveying.
   d. *inclusion*: one token in the tie refers to a member or a component of the entity referred to in the other token, e.g. 'investigators', 'Jones'. The category of inclusion includes hyponymy, meronymy and superordination.

We considered lexical ties only if they were across sentences or across clauses separated by a semi-colon. Each tie between a lexical item and the lexical item that it linked back to constituted a 'tie'. In turn, each tie was classified by the above taxonomy. Citations to literature that were outside clause structure were excluded.

In the Introduction and Discussion sections of the articles in the corpus, repetition and synonymy account for 99 per cent of the cohesive links. The only ties created by inclusion are the ties between generic terms such as 'investigators' and the names of specific individuals, and ties among 'hypothesis', 'premise', 'rationale'. Although these latter words have specific non-inclusive meanings, they are often used rather loosely, such that there are inclusive lexical relations among them.

How lexical cohesion functions

Having outlined the parameters of the study, we can now move on to examine the use of lexical cohesion in the corpus of SSR articles. In the first section (Words and genre), we relate the use of lexical cohesion to the research article genre. In the second (Patterns of words), we illustrate the connection between lexical cohesion and semiotic organization of the articles in the Introduction and Discussion sections and within individual moves in those sections. The third section of the findings (Lexical cohesion and social context) relates lexical cohesion to the interpersonal aspects of the research articles.

Words and genre

There is a bi-directional connection between lexical cohesion and genre. On the one hand, lexical choices including cohesion instantiate or realize the genre. On the other hand, the genre predicts the use of particular lexis. Below, we focus firstly on the research related lexical items in the current genre, and in the following section specify the lexical items that participate in the cohesive chains.

Choices of words

All the lexical items in the research narrative strand of Introductions and Discussions (i.e. other than lexis based on the specific phenomena under study) were organized into systems and the related features (shown in Figure 5.3). The combination of the features into a taxonomy provides the range of possible realizations for a feature and sets out the relationship between various lexical items. For example, 'Jones and Smith' and 'Jones and colleagues' share the features [producer: identified: outsiders] but differ in the feature [equal].

The lexical choices in our corpus represent a small selection from the total options in the language. To take one example, the process 'theorize' has nineteen synonyms in the corpus (see Figure 5.3) compared to 47 synonyms in *Roget's Thesaurus* (Lloyd, 1986). Authors never 'claim', 'guess' or 'suppose' in the corpus. Rather, in this genre of academic discourse, they 'argue', 'speculate' and 'hypothesize'. There are also finer grained distinctions. For example, even within the semantic set of 'theorizing', the feature [not firm] is chosen. As we suggested in Chapter 4, authors of SSR articles rarely use 'conclude', and do so only if the agent is not the current author, another interpersonal characteristic of this genre.

Although there is a tradition that sees lexical choices as governed by discrete categories of field, mode and tenor, the taxonomy of semantic features in Figure 5.3 shows that the boundaries of field, mode and tenor are not clear-cut. For

example, while hedging structures may stem from clearly interpersonal considerations such as politeness or the need for objectivity, they also may implicate field
or mode considerations. In particular, factive verbs are avoided when authors
report their own work in social science, which is not the convention in molecular
genetics (Myers, 1992, as we reported in Chapter 3, Move 3 of Introductions).
It is possible that such choices, which originally reflected selections of tenor (e.g.
politeness, modesty), have been institutionalized in the choices that now help
form the mode values in research journal articles. Young (1990: 180) also found
this in her study of academic spoken discourse, where there was not necessarily
a 'neat' one-to-one correspondence between each registerial construct and lexical
or structural choice. The overlap seemed then and continues to seem not
unusual when we consider that language occurs in a situation in which there is
a network of interacting relationships.

Another factor in the formation of the genre of research articles is the use of
the features [animate] and [inanimate]. The genre seems to humanize inanimate
elements while keeping the animate author less prominent. In constructing the
taxonomy of features for research articles, we found that the distinction of
animate/inanimate for agents cuts across categories established in the taxonomy
(Figure 5.3). No category of 'process' is restricted to either human or inanimate
agents, although there may be some restrictions within the category. For
example, within the category of 'state', both inanimate and human agents
'report', but only humans 'note' and only inanimate agents 'document' (Table
5.1). Human agents mainly perform intellectual activities. Nevertheless, seemingly inanimate 'studies' can 'consider', 'observe', 'examine' and 'compare' (see
column labelled BOTH). In fact, even creative thought processes may have an
inanimate agent, such as 'the data suggest'. But animate actors, that is the
authors or researchers, tend not to appear directly. Rather, by making inanimate
elements animate and, therefore, more human, the facts are presented as
speaking for themselves with the authors in the background. As Gilbert and
Mulkay (1984) put it, 'Empiricist discourse is organized in a manner which
denies its character as an interpretive product and which denies that its authors'
actions are relevant to its content' (quoted in Swales, 1990: 123).

Word after word: the making of chains

The following eight categories represent the lexical items that form chains of
three or more items in the Introductions and Discussions:

Research: included are lexical items that share the semantic field of
research; most such items are products of the research process, e.g. *study*,
but also included is the process itself, e.g. *examine*

Theory: products of reasoning, e.g. conclusion

Theorize: processes of reasoning

Problem: defects or scarcity in research

Results: lexical items which share the semantic field of results

Figure 5.3 Taxonomy of lexical choices

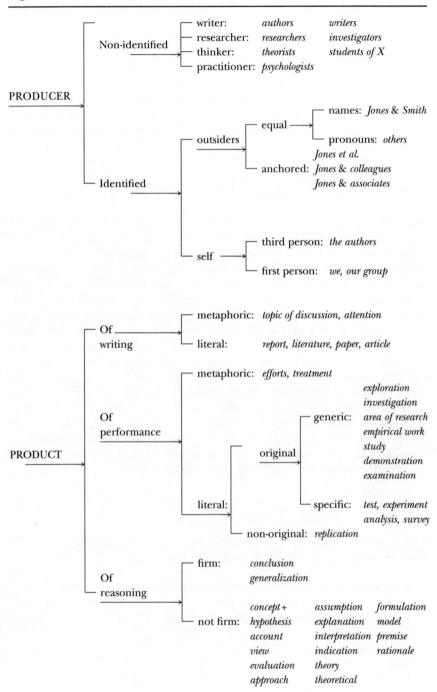

Figure 5.3 (*continued*)

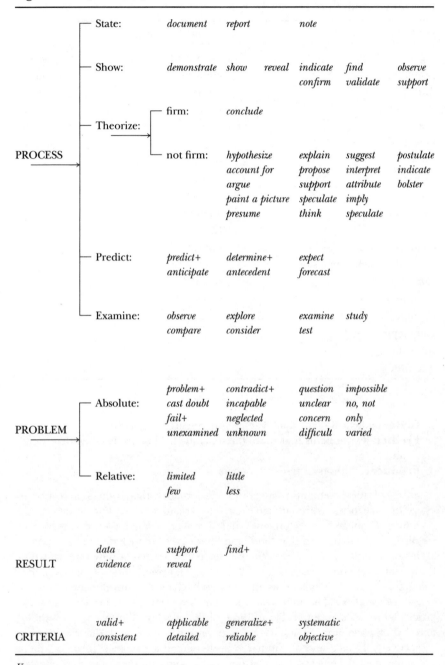

State:	*document*	*report*	*note*		
Show:	*demonstrate*	*show*	*reveal*	*indicate*	*find*	*observe*
				confirm	*validate*	*support*

Theorize:

firm:	*conclude*				
not firm:	*hypothesize*	*explain*	*suggest*	*postulate*
	account for	*propose*	*interpret*	*indicate*
	argue	*support*	*attribute*	*bolster*
	paint a picture	*speculate*	*imply*	
	presume	*think*	*speculate*	

Predict:

predict+	*determine+*	*expect*
anticipate	*antecedent*	*forecast*

Examine:

observe	*explore*	*examine*	*study*
compare	*consider*	*test*	

PROCESS

PROBLEM

Absolute:

problem+	*contradict+*	*question*	*impossible*
cast doubt	*incapable*	*unclear*	*no, not*
fail+	*neglected*	*concern*	*only*
unexamined	*unknown*	*difficult*	*varied*

Relative:

limited	*little*
few	*less*

RESULT

data	*support*	*find+*
evidence	*reveal*	

CRITERIA

valid+	*applicable*	*generalize+*	*systematic*
consistent	*detailed*	*reliable*	*objective*

Key
+ = other forms of same lexeme; italicized items = realizations

Table 5.1 Processes of performing, analysing and reporting research and indicating strength of results, by type of agent

Human agent only	Inanimate only	Both
argue	document	report
propose	confirm	observe
find	bolster	show
demonstrate	focus	consider
test	provide	examine
hypothesize	suggest	compare
think	support	explain
explore	imply	
note	predict	
anticipate	attempt	
expect	hold	
conduct	indicate	
conclude, reach conclusion	yield	
study	reveal	
determine	account for	
attempt		
paint a picture		
speculate		
interpret		

Criteria: lexical items that evaluate the research, e.g. consistent

Predict: lexical items that share the semantic field of predict, e.g. determine, and

Producer: authors of research papers

Some of these semantic categories are broader than others in order to establish categories with enough items to create chains. For instance, the preliminary categories of 'process' and 'product' related to the category of 'results' were collapsed so that 'find' and 'findings' were included in one chain.

In some semantic categories, the tokens mainly represent only one or two of the possible options (see Tables 5.2 and 5.3 for the range of options). For example, of the 119 tokens in the 'research chain in Introductions', 81 are 'study' or 'studies'. The more specific term 'experiments' is used in only one article, although it is applicable to three of the articles. The tokens 'hypothesis' and 'hypothesize' appear only three times (in the 'theory' and 'theorize' chains, respectively; Texts 5 and 6). Similarly, in the semantic category 'theorize', there are some typical choices of lexical items and some infrequently used choices. 'Suggest' is used for half the occurrences of the 'theorize' category in the

Introduction and Discussion sections (Tables 5.2 and 5.3). In the related 'theory' category in Discussions, 'explanations' account for 30, 'theory' for seventeen and 'interpretation' for six of the total 86 realizations. These realizations also select the [not firm] feature and may represent the most hedged choices; the choices would then again be constrained by interpersonal intentions.

In the 'producer' chain, 'we' is included, although it is not a clearly lexical item from an open class grammatical category, because 'we' in these research texts refers to the members of the class 'researchers', which is central to the 'researchers' lexical chain (Table 5.2). (See Martin, 1992, for a parallel argument.)

Next, we consider whether cohesion is sensitive to generic structures. Firstly, below, lexical cohesion in the Introductions is compared to that of the Discussions in those same articles. Then the use of lexical cohesion in the different moves within each section is investigated.

Patterns of words in Introductions and Discussions

The Introduction and Discussion sections of SSR articles each have characteristic patterns of lexical choices. Firstly, the Introductions are richer in the variety of processes realized. (Table 5.4 shows the total range.) This difference may be due to the fact that the research narrative strand is more prominent in Introductions. Secondly, in Discussion sections, the most varied category among the processes is 'theorize', reflecting the interpretation role of Discussions. Interestingly, processes that represent the authors' lack of conviction in the propositions they report (e.g. 'paint a picture', 'presume', 'speculate', 'suspect', 'think', 'argue') are used only in Introductions (where other authors' ideas are highlighted).

In the 'Problem' chain, there are differences in the two sections reflecting different generic elements. In the Introductions, the generic element of 'establishing the gap' is realized lexically by items denoting scarcity of research (e.g. 'few') nine out of 26 times. In contrast, in the Discussion sections, items of scarcity are not used, since the generic structure element is not 'establish the gap' but rather 'ward off counterclaims'. This latter generic structure element anticipates problems in the research being reported rather than outlining problems in other researchers' work. For similar reasons, perhaps, the use of 'fail' in the 'problem' chain is different in Introductions and Discussions. 'Fail' is used more in Discussions (seven out of 21) than in Introductions (two of 26). As may be expected, the longest 'problem' chain, both in absolute length and relative to other chains, is found in Text 1 in which all the results that are reported were contrary to the researchers' expectations.

There are other differences between the Introduction and Discussion sections that reflect the functions of these two sections. Introductions are realized by processes that relate to the gathering of data (Process chain) but these processes are rare in Discussion sections. On the other hand, Discussions, but not Introductions, emphasize interpretation of data and so are realized by a richer

Table 5.2 Lexical cohesion choices in Introductions, by move (Texts 1–8 combined)

MOVE	RESEARCH PRODUCT	N	PROCESS	N	THEORY	N	THEORIZE	N	PROBLEM	N	RESULTS	N	CRITERIA	N	PREDICT	N	PRODUCER	N
1	study	28	show	3	theory	3	suggest	4			evidence	6	valid	2	predict	10	P&W	1
	research	6	observe	2	approach	2	conclude	3			find	5	generalizable	1	expect	6	Investigators	3
	investigation	2	demonstrate	2	conceptions	1	explain	1			results	2			anticipate	4	C & F	1
	analysis	1	test	1	conclusion	1	argue	1			data	1			forecast	3	C et al.	1
	empirical work	1	reveal	1	formulation	1	hypothesize	1			support	1			antecedent	1	F	1
	experiments	1	indicate	1	theoretical	1	paint a picture	1									F & K	1
	literature	1	identify	1	view	1	presume	1									H & assoc	1
	set of papers	1	explore	1			propose	1									H, G & G	1
	surveys	1	document	1			suspect	1									Jasso	1
	topic	1	consider	1			think	1									L, C & assoc	1
	treatment	1																
2	study	19	examine	2	theories	2	suggest	4	problem	4	data	2					investigators	2
	research	3	focus	2	concepts	2	attribute	1	little	3	results	1					A et al.	1
	test	3	observe	2	generalizations	1	explain	1	concern	2							P & W	1
	reports	2	confirm	1			presume	1	fail	2							P & assoc	1
	attention	1	consider	1					only one [study]	2								
	efforts	1	note	1					impossible	1								
	work	1	report	1					limited	1								
			test	1					no	1								
									no [studies]	1								
									not [adj]	1								
									not well [adj]	1								
									unexamined	1								
									unknown	1								
									varied	1								
3	study	34	conduct	4	conclusion	1	suggest	1	difficult	4	results	5	detailed	1			we	4
	research	4	examine	3	hypotheses	1	conclude	2	few	1	evidence	3	systematic	1			F et al.	2
	investigation	3	report	3	premise	1	indicate	2	less	1	find	7	objective	1			Investigators	2
	analyses	1	provides	2	rationale	1	speculate	1	neglect	1	data	1	valid	2			Bronfen.	1
	applications	1	confirm	1	theoretical	1							generalizable	1			Ladd	1
	article	1	demonstrate	1													M & F	1
	attention	1	explore	1													M & N	1
	efforts	1	observe	1													N, N & N	1
	here	1	reveal	1													W et al.	1
	literature	1	study	1													students	1
	paper	1																
	replicate	1																
	survey	1																

Key Move 1, claim relevance; Move 2, establish gap; Move 3, preview authors' contribution; N = number

Table 5.3 Lexical cohesion choices in Discussions, by move (Texts 1–8 combined)

	RESEARCH																	
MOVE	PRODUCT	N	PROCESS	N	THEORY	N	THEORIZE	N	PROBLEM	N	RESULTS	N	CRITERIA	N	PREDICT	N	PRODUCER	N
	study	20	report	9	theoretical	3	suggest	5	fail	2	result	9	valid	1	predictively			
	research	3	examine	1	interpretation	1	explain	1	limited	1	finding	6	validated	1	predictor	7		
A	investigation	2	test	1	conclusion	1			cast doubt	1	found	5	validity	1				
	attention	1									data	2						
	report	1									evidence	2						
											reveal	2						
	study	27	study	2	hypothesis	5	suggest	2	fail	1	results	8	consistent	9	predictions	2		
	report	4	replicate	1	conceptualization	1					finding	4	validate	4	determinants	1		
B	survey	3									found	2	generalizable	2	predictors	1		
	replication	2									data	1	reliable	2				
	experiments	1									reveal	1						
	research	1																
	study	10			explanation	17	suggest	10	failure	3	found	21	consistent	5				
	analysis	2			hypothesis	4	explain	4			result	13						
	report	2			formulation	2	hypothesize	2			data	4						
C	examination	1			accounts	1	bolster	1			evidence	3						
	search	1			interpretation	1	indicating	1			finding	3						
	test	1					interpret	1										
							support	1										
	study	19			explanation	13	account	7	problem	4	results	12	valid	9	predict	3	Harvey	1
	analysis	4			theory	5	explain	6	failure	1	finding	9	generalizability	2	determination	1	Walker	1
D	report	2			interpretation	4	suggest	5	limited	1	found	1	reliable	1			investigators	1
	investigation	1			hypothesis	1	conclude	2	contradictor	1	support	1					researchers	1
	research	1					interpret	1	difficulty	1	data	3						
									incapable	1	evidence	1						
	study	16	explore	1	theories	8	suggest	12	neglected	1	data	7	consistent	2	determinants	1	Caplan	1
	research	10	investigate	1	view	4	explain	3	question	1	findings	6	applicable	1	determination	1	Freud	1
	analysis	3			conception	3	indicate	2	unclear	1	results	6	inconsistencies	1	predictions	1	Parke & W	1
	investigation	3			model	3	imply	1			evidence	3			predictive	1	investigators	1
E	article	1			approach	2	postulate	1			information	2			predictors	1	researchers	1
	attention	1			formulation	2											theorists	1
	demonstration	1			assumption	1											writers	1
	examination	1			indication	1												
	test	1			postulate	1												

Key Move A, report accomplishments; Move B, evaluate congruence; Move C, offer interpretation; Move D, ward off counterclaims; Move E, state implications; N = number

Table 5.4 Processes by occurrence in Introduction and Discussion sections

State	Show	Theorize	Examine	Predict
		Introduction		
document	show	suggest	observe*	anticipate
report	demonstrate	conclude	explore	expect
note	reveal	reach conclusion	examine	forecast
present	indicate	explain	compare	predict
	find	argue	consider	attribute
	confirm	hypothesize	test	
	validate	propose	study	
	support	think	attempt to discover	
	point to	paint a picture		
	observe*	suspect		
		speculate		
		presume		
		Discussion		
report	find	interpret	test	predict
	account for	bolster	study	expect
	imply	hold		
		not rule out		
		recommend**		
		postulate		
		suggest		
		conclude		
		explain		
		hypothesize		

Notes
* 'observe' is used in at least two senses: 'to find' as in 'We have observed no evidence to support the hypothesis' (Text 5) and 'to examine' as in 'We are unaware of prior studies that directly observed the more relevant phenomena of anxiety . . .' (Text 3).
** i.e. authors prefer an interpretation.

'theorize' chain, as mentioned above. At a more delicate level of analysis, 'producer' is not found in Moves A, B and C in Discussions (results, congruence and interpretation) but is found in all three moves of the Introductions.

Other chains also are distributed variably depending on the section and move they help to realize. The 'research' chain is found in all Introduction and Discussion sections (Table 5.5). Since the Introduction emphasizes reviewing

Table 5.5 Distribution of cohesive chains, by text and section

Chain	Text 1 ID	Text 2 ID	Text 3 ID	Text 4 ID	Text 5 ID	Text 6 ID	Text 7 ID	Text 8 ID	Number of texts in which chain appears I	D
Theory	✓✓	✓✓	–✓	–✓	––	✓✓	–✓	✓✓	4	7
Theorize	–✓	✓✓	✓✓	✓✓	✓–	✓✓	–✓	✓✓	6	7
Research	✓✓	✓✓	✓✓	✓✓	✓✓	✓✓	✓✓	✓✓	8	8
Producer	✓–	✓–	––	––	✓–	✓–	✓–	✓✓	6	1
Results	–✓	–✓	✓✓	✓✓	✓✓	✓✓	✓✓	✓✓	6	8
Problem	–✓	✓✓	✓✓	–✓	––	––	––	✓✓	3	5
Criteria	––	–✓	✓✓	––	––	–✓	–✓	–✓	1	5
Predict	––	–✓	––	––	––	✓✓	––	––	1	2

Key: I = Introduction; D = Discussion; – = chain absent; ✓ = chain present

previous literature we find 'producer' more prominent in the Introductions and least prominent in Discussions. In fact, the only Discussion section that includes a 'producer' (Text 8) very strongly challenges previous literature. The 'results' chain is found in all discussion sections since it represents the discourse topic of these sections, e.g. the results are ... , the results are consistent with ... , the explanation of the results is ... The next most frequent chains are 'theory' and 'theorize'. The frequency of these chains may be due to the fact that they can be realized in the moves of 'offer interpretation', and 'ward off counterclaims' within the Discussion section. Similarly, the use of the 'criteria' chain once in the Introductions but five times in the Discussions is consistent with the reflection of the generic structure element of evaluating congruence, which is a component of Discussions.

Patterns of words in specific moves

There is not a strong relationship between lexical choices within chains, types and distribution of chains, and genre structure (i.e. moves), except for the expected 'problem' string in Move 2 ('establish the gap') (Table 5.2) and Move D ('ward off counterclaims') (Table 5.3). That is, the unit of move does not correlate clearly with the use of lexical chains of three or more items (see Tables 5.2, 5.3). This finding parallels Ventola's (1987) conclusion that, in the genre of service encounters, the ranges of lexical strings could not be correlated with the hypothesized general structure. We will return to the reasons for both findings below.

In the SSR texts, some lexical chains extend through more than one move. For example, in the Introductions, the 'problem' chain is most conspicuous in Move 2, 'establish the gap', but can also extend to Move 3, 'preview the authors' contribution'. Similarly, the 'problems' lexical chain is found in the Introduction but also reappears in the Discussion section as stating the problems that the authors tried to resolve.

There may, though, be several reasons for the lack of correspondence between lexical cohesion and the moves that construct the generic structure. The brevity of the texts and of moves in particular may not enable the construction of lexical chains. A writing style that avoids certain kinds of embedded sentences, e.g. 'People like to read (Jones and Smith, 1999)' instead of 'Jones and Smith (1999) claim that people like to read' may also lead to shorter sentences and shorter lexical chains. Another reason for the lack of correspondence between moves and lexical cohesion involves the definition of a move as composed of different acts. The head act in a move is obligatory, but there may be other subsidiary acts of various kinds and lengths within a single type of move. For example, Move 2, 'establish the gap', may consist of the one obligatory act or may also include several other acts of reviewing the scientific literature. These acts would then realize the chains relevant to them, rather than to the head act.

Lexical cohesion and social context

In the section 'Patterns of words in Introductions and Discussions' (p. 115), we outlined the relationship of vocabulary choices to the overall genre of social science research texts and in the next section the relationship of lexis to the more specific semiological organization of the texts. We can now turn to the ways in which the interpersonal or social context influences vocabulary choice.

In any text, including the research texts being examined, the three functions of language – ideational, interpersonal and textual – are woven together as the text unfolds. Specifically, in these research texts, the 'facts' of the phenomena being presented are fashioned into a narrative that describes how the facts were uncovered and the author's attitude towards these facts. The third function, the textual, creates a semantic and textual unity that enables the other two kinds of functions to be expressed. The text in Figure 5.4 realizes the ideational function by presenting facts as in Move 1 (e.g. 'Previous studies have shown . . .'), the interpersonal function by indicating the authors' purpose (e.g. to convince the reader that the topic of the study is relevant, that a gap exists, and that the present research contributes towards filling that gap), and the textual function partly by distributing given and new information and conforming to elements of a narrative schema (see Chapter 3). However, a text may contain elements of these three functions and still seem rather disjointed. In the text in Figure 5.4, we show how chains of lexical cohesion (in boldface) help to delicately mesh the three functions.

In the text in Figure 5.4, intersentential ties create the following chains of at least three nominal groups:

    a. time: the time-frame of the research narrative is narrowed from 'the past decade' to 'recent studies' to the current time ('here' which in fact also

Figure 5.4   Lexical cohesion chains in sample text

Nominal groups with lexical cohesion are highlighted

MOVE I: CLAIM RELEVANCE OF FIELD

#1.   Over **the past decade**, **many investigators** have called for a closer analysis
of the language learning environment of the young infant (e.g. N*).
2. Within **the recent rapid proliferation of studies** of infant audition (. . .)
an area of research has emerged to identify those stimulus parameters that
best attract the attention of the young infant and that may contribute to
early language learning. 3. **Previous studies** have shown that young infants
will selectively attend to novel and familiar auditory stimuli (Name and
Name) . . . 5. **Recent studies** show that increased pitch variability . . .
(N, N) typify adult-to-infant vocalizations. 9. In fact, the effect of various
intonation patterns on infant attention has been explored in **a few studies**.
10. **Sullivan and Horowitz** (1983) tested the salience of rising versus falling
intonation contour . . . 11. **Two other studies conducted by Fernald** have
shown that . . . 12. **Fernald and Kuhl** have also shown selectivity . . .

MOVE II: ESTABLISH THE GAP THE PRESENT RESEARCH IS MEANT TO FILL

13.   **Aslin** *et al.* . . . note that the exact factors responsible for this apparent
salience . . . remain undetermined.

MOVE III: PREVIEW THE AUTHORS' CONTRIBUTION

[No new para.] 14. **We** report **here the results of three studies** on one parameter
of adult-to-infant speech, **studies** in which **we** have observed no evidence to
support the hypothesis that frequency modulation *per se* constitutes a salient
feature of the infant's acoustic environment. (Text 5)

\# Sentence number
* Name of researcher

represents the time of 'now'); this narrowing coalesces with the authors'
need to establish relevance;
  b. research products: the cohesive chain narrows the focus from a rather
broad 'proliferation' of studies to the one study being presented by the
authors (represented by 'here');
  c. researchers: in conformity with the research narrative, the agents represented in the nominal group are narrowed down from an anonymous
community of scholars ('many investigators') to the heroes of the subsequent story, authors of the current study (realized as 'we').

This narrowing is part of the research narrative and represents an increase in
interaction between author and reader, thus a change in the interpersonal

function. The changes in the 'time' and 'research products' chains also mirror this change in interpersonal function, with a closer relationship being created between author and reader. Each lexical chain, then, narrows the focus, with each chain ending with the current authors in direct relationship with the reader through the text. Thus the ideational elements of 'research products' and 'researchers', the interpersonal function of relation between author and reader and the textual function of lexical cohesion are woven together to create the texture of the research article and establish it as a member of its genre.

Summary

Our analysis of lexical cohesion of the research strand in eight SSR texts shows that texts of a single genre seem to use the same cohesive building blocks. This leads to a similarity and unity across the texts of this genre. There are a number of reasons for this conclusion: (1) the lexical chains in the various texts draw their realizations from a limited group of lexical items (Figure 5.3), (2) the lexical choices in these chains belong to a limited set of eight semantic categories, and (3) the lexical ties in the chains are almost always based on repetition and synonymy. This concentration on these two types of lexical tie reflects the fact that scientific texts tend to use resources aimed at clarity and definition. In contrast, analyses that are based primarily on oral and/or narrative texts (Fine, 1978, 1994; Hasan, 1984; Martin, as cited by Ventola, 1987: 132; Yang, 1989) have revealed a greater variety of lexical cohesion, which may be due to the fact that precision is not as significant a factor in non-scientific genres and, therefore, the need to rely only on synonymy and repetition is reduced.

In relating lexical cohesion to the genre units of research articles, we found no correspondence between lexical cohesion and moves, but did find a relationship with the more macro level units of Introductions and Discussions. Although the Introduction sections and Discussion sections draw from the same lexical categories, there is a different selection of specific lexical items, reflecting the different rhetorical functions of Introductions. For instance, since Discussions point to deficiencies in the present research while Introductions can also highlight scarcity in previous research, the realizations 'few' and 'rare' occur in the 'problem' chain of Introductions only. The lack of correspondence between lexical cohesion and the unit of move is probably due to the relatively short length of moves and their composition of various acts that makes them functionally heterogeneous.

In the search for more abstract concepts that may influence lexical cohesion, field, mode and tenor have been proposed as categories that reflect social reality and from which register is delineated (see above and Chapter 1). In this view, a phrase such as 'the data suggest' would be controlled by field (research), 'this paper' by mode (journal article), and 'we' and 'other researchers' largely by tenor. However, using 'the data' as the agent of 'suggest' instead of 'we', for example, creates empiricist discourse, which hides the authors as the interpreters of fact. The use of the process 'suggest' encodes the features of non-contention and modest conviction about the truth value of the proposition. Thus, social relationships work to shape choices of field. In fact, the configurations of field and interpersonal choices then become identified with certain institutionalized forms of communication in a specific channel of communication, so that even the mode seems shaped by choices of field. It may be that the appropriate realization for each move is a subset of the realizations deriving from the corresponding register for the genre and macro unit (such as Discussion or Introduction). The specific communicative purposes of each move further constrain the semantic features and their realizations. Whether such a more specific relationship holds for moves must be determined by further research. But within the boundaries of our current work, we can examine and delineate another type of dependency structure that also relates entities vertically, that of reference, to better understand how the participants (people, places and things identified by the author) are kept track of through the course of an article. This is the focus of Chapter 6.

6 The cast of characters in scientific texts

Background: relating participants to events

Several interdependent structural strata are needed to characterize a genre. There are structures consisting of constituents that each account for a discrete section of the text. These structures may be seen as horizontal structures. These horizontal structures have been described earlier (Chapters 3 and 4) in terms of the moves and rhetorical structures of social science research texts. In addition to these systems of constituents, there are dependency relations that run through a text. For these dependency relations, the meaning of an item is retrievable from another item in the string of items. These strings of items, e.g. pronouns or definite nominal groups ('the findings'), can be seen as vertical relations through a text that help bind the text into an entity that is interpretable with continuous elements of meaning running through it. In Chapter 5, we saw how continuity of meaning is maintained by selecting lexical items from specific lexical sets and how the chains of lexical items create unity in the text. In the current chapter, we deal with the discourse system of reference that establishes who the actors and objects are in a text. As Martin (1992: 95) phrased it, we must account for getting 'people, places and things into a text and referring to them once there'.

Systems to refer to participants

What are participants?

Several interrelated distinctions are needed to build up the reference systems that keep track of participants in a discourse. The reference systems lead to the use of different signals to track participants and signal chains of dependencies in the text. The requirement to start a reference to an entity is the presence of a participant, defined by Martin (1992: 129) as 'a person, place or thing, abstract or concrete, capable of functioning as Agent [an external cause for a process] or Medium [entity through which a process is realized] in Transitivity [the organization of participants and processes in language]'. As well as the persons, places and things that are available to the speech community, new participants can be readily created by grammatical metaphor. (See Halliday, 1997, for a discussion.)

For example, from the verb 'to implement', a participant 'implementation' can be created. A complex phenomenon can also be made into a participant. Halliday and Hasan (1976: 52) give the example of an eye-witness description of an accident. The entire accident can then be turned into a participant by saying '*It* all happened so quickly'. In this and other cases, the participant need not be a nominal group like 'the idea', 'the young child', or 'the similarity in the hypotheses' but may be a large portion of text that is later referred to by a pronoun – '*That* is necessary'. On the other hand, some nominals do not signal the presence of a participant, e.g. empty 'it' ('It is not important that he go'). As these examples show, the mere presence or absence of a nominal group cannot be directly taken as the presence or absence of a participant.

The semantic features of participants

As a starting point for identifying features that specify the participants in the social science research texts, we turn to Martin (1992), who has clarified many features that distinguish participants in reference networks. We will focus only on those that are needed to understand the participant relations in the research articles.

1. Phoric or non-phoric: This distinction conveys whether the nominal group identifies the participant as recoverable (phoric), e.g. 'the bicycle', or non-recoverable (non-phoric), e.g. 'bicycles', in the text.
2. Presenting or presuming: Presenting reference introduces new participants and signals that the identity of the participant cannot be recovered from the context. Presuming reference signals that the identity of the participant can be recovered. This presuming reference can be created by using phoric items that require the reader to presume information from the context (see Martin, 1992: 98–102). In the unfolding of a text, presenting references (e.g. 'an idea') are used with the first mention of a participant and presuming references ('it') are used when mentioning the same participant later.
3. Generic or specific reference: Generic references select out the whole of a class of participants instead of a specific subset of the class (specific reference). In the following example from Martin (1992: 103), the generic references to deserts are in bold and the specific references are underlined:

   > Fifteen per cent of the world's land area consists of **deserts. The true hot deserts** straddle the Tropics in both hemispheres. **They** are found on all continents . . . **Cool deserts** are found further polewards . . . There are five major hot desert belts in the world . . . The largest hot desert extends from the west coast of North Africa . . . This is the great Sahara . . .

4. Location of identifying information: Information needed to identify a participant that is signalled by a phoric nominal group may be found in various locations (the following distinctions are derived from Halliday and Hasan, 1976, and Martin, 1992).

a) Exophora: Exophora is reference to information outside the text itself. This information may be assumed to be generally available, e.g. '**The sun** sets at seven in the evening'; '**The literature** states that . . .'. On the other hand, exophoric reference may instruct the reader to find information outside the text in the situation of the language event, e.g. '**We** think that **you** should take **this book** home' (for which 'we', 'you' and 'this book' require information from the non-verbal context).

b) Endophora: Endophora is reference to some other stretch of language: that is the identity of the participant referred to by endophora can be determined from the text itself. There are numerous systems that detail various kinds of endophora; here we introduce only those distinctions that play a role in our analysis of the research texts. The search for identifying information in a text may involve:

   i) a prior part of the text (anaphora), e.g. 'Adam found an apple. **He** ate **it**', in which the identity of 'he' and 'it' are retrievable from 'Adam' and 'an apple'.

   ii) a following part of the text (cataphora), e.g. '**This** is what I want to explain to you. First take the square bracket . . .' in which 'This' points to a following part of the text.

   iii) the text in the given nominal group (esphora), e.g. 'the man I saw yesterday', in which the identity of 'the man' is given within the nominal group.

Related to the location of the information that endophora refers to is the extent of the information that identifies the participant mentioned in the endophoric reference. The identifying information may simply be a nominal group as in the example of 'Adam' and 'the apple', above, or the identifying information may be a reference to a larger piece of text as in the example of the eye-witness report later referred to as 'It' in 'It happened so quickly'.

In sum, we have described the participants and the semantic features that can be used to refer to the participants as the texts proceeds. We can now present some of the general findings about the presentation of participants in the research texts and how these texts reflect the specific genre. We will describe how the participants in the research articles are identified and tracked.

Reference networks in operation

There is evidence that various registers and genres are characterized by the patterns of reference that track the participants. For example, children's play-groups and other highly knit social groups show relatively great amounts of exophoric reference (Halliday and Hasan, 1976). Similarly, in service encounters, the majority of references are exophoric rather than endophoric (Ventola, 1987). In fact, 'the very disarray of reference chains [representing the items to be bought], the lack of participant 'heroes' is the best indication of the realization of the generic structure elements' (Ventola, 1989: 158). In terms of register, in contrast to genre (as detailed above), Fine (1994: 178–80) shows that there are different patterns of reference in students' conversations depending upon whether or not a teacher was present.

As mentioned above, participants can be created by nominalization. This method of presenting participants is especially associated with abstract written English in science, humanities and administration (Martin, 1992: 138). Such texts, according to Martin, typically involve generic as opposed to specific reference, so that few of the nominalized participants are linked in long chains of reference. Rather, esophoric reference is common, directing the reader to interpret the identity of the participant from within the nominal group (e.g. 'the implementation of key targets').

Another example of reference helping to characterize a genre is given by Brown and Yule (1983). They make a distinction between participants that refer to other participants more than one nominal group away (displaced entities) and participants that refer to the participant in the immediately preceding nominal group (current entities). In one genre, directions for diagram drawing, displaced entities are always referred to by a definite referring expression (the + noun), often with an identifying property (the + property + noun). Such entities in the genre are never referred to by pronouns or by ellipsis. Pronouns, when they occur in the genre, only identify current entities, i.e. participants in the immediately preceding nominal group (Brown and Yule, 1983: 174). In contrast, in the recipes genre, they found participants tracked through ellipsis even when the antecedent was more than one nominal group away, e.g. 'Let the dough rise in a greased bowl until double in bulk. Form into sticks or pretzels. Place on a greased sheet'.

Our method for studying reference relations among participants is similar to the method we used to identify lexical chains (Chapter 5). All participants in the research narrative strand of the Introductions and Discussions in eight articles were analysed. 'Participant' was defined as a nominal group that can function as Medium or Agent. For example, in the sentence 'In this article, we explain that early school experience . . .', the nominal groups 'this article' and 'we' are included in the analysis. Only participants realized syntactically or in parentheses were included. That is, elided or deleted nominal groups and participants appearing only in footnotes were excluded. After a preliminary analysis of all such strings of participants, we concentrated on the three major participants common to the majority of the texts: past research, present research and problems.

Who/what are the participants in the network?

As expected, there are major differences between scientific texts and the oral narrative genre described, *inter alia*, in Martin (1992). Whereas ordinary narratives centre around a few participants that extend throughout the full text and interact with each other, research texts are composed of many participants that traverse short portions of the text and keep their separate identities. The diversity of participants reflects the multiple stories that an author is telling in the literature review of a research article. There is not one 'hero' as in a narrative, but a collection of brief stories each with its central participants or heroes. Another difference between narratives and scientific texts is that very few of the participants realized syntactically are animate. Even the present authors are sometimes realized as products and not as producers, e.g. *this study*, as we show below. However, the present authors are usually expressed at least once by a personal pronoun (often, 'we') and are the only participants that traverse both the Introduction and Discussion sections. In contrast, other individuals are prominent in the research articles only if they are the focus of a debate, e.g. 'Cohen argues . . .' (Text 2), and are almost never referred to by a personal pronoun. The present authors, then, as the major participants, are tracked differently from other participants in the research narrative strand.

In both Introductions and Discussions, the three densest reference chains refer to present research, past research and problems. Of these, only 'present research' tracks a single participant. The entity of 'past research' is composed of many different participants that form short micro-chains within past research. In the following example, each paragraph has a short chain of a participant (indicated in bold) that does not extend to other paragraphs. Sentence numbers are given to indicate the extent of the material deleted.

Paragraph I
    4. **A number of studies** have documented tobacco withdrawal phenomena. 5. However, the validity and generalizability of **these studies** may be limited. 6. One of the concerns about the validity of **the studies** is that most relied on self-reported symptoms that may have been inaccurate . . .
Paragraph II
    12. **Systematic prospective studies** . . . would prevent both the problems of self retrospective designs. 13. **Such studies** are common in the fields of alcohol, sedative, and opiate withdrawal. 14. However, **similar studies** for tobacco withdrawal have only recently been completed by our group and others. 15. **These inpatient studies** confirmed most self-reported withdrawal symptoms. 16. In addition, **our study** reported that subjects have few withdrawal symptoms as inpatients . . . 17. This result suggests that environmental cues (e.g. other smokers) are crucial . . .
Paragraph III
    18. A final concern with **studies** on tobacco withdrawal is that several important facets of the disorder have not been well described. 19. For example, **reports** of the severity, duration, and time course of tobacco withdrawal are quite varied. 20. Also, why some smokers have severe withdrawal symptoms and others have minimal symptoms is unknown (Text 3).

In the Introductions, 'past research' is the most frequent participant and is expressed by the short micro-chains mentioned earlier. 'Present research' is the next most frequent participant. In contrast to the Introductions, however, in Discussions the most frequent participant and the only one found in all the articles is a chain of present research. In these discussions, references to past research are individual references or chains of only two items. The result is that the 'past research' participants appear as minor entities compared to the participants of the present research, which dominate the Discussion sections. The density and kinds of participants tracked by the reference systems mirror the rhetorical functions of the Introductions and Discussions.

In another example of how participants are expressed in particular genre structures, human participants are rarely realized in Move 2, 'establish the gap'. If human participants are realized then, they are only presented as the perceiver of the gap, e.g. 'Aslin *et al.* note that [X] is undetermined' (Text 5). The effect of these linguistic patterns is to generalize as opposed to particularizing the criticism of previous scientific literature (see also the discussion of Move 2, in Chapter 3).

Keeping track of participants

SSR articles introduce various participants, as they have been defined in the previous section. The next consideration is how these participants are drawn through the texts such that the reader can continually recognize the same participants as they reappear in the texts. The chains of these participants can be compared to different coloured threads that are pulled through a piece of cloth. The thread will weave in and out of the background cloth and the observer's eye is drawn to the special colour and recognizes the thread each time it reappears. The specific question is 'How are the different participants signalled through the research articles?' The simple answer is that different participants are signalled in different ways in different sections of the articles.

The systems of reference in English include both exophoric reference that points outside the text itself (such as 'we' and 'you') and references to within the text (such as 'they' and 'it'). However, in the research texts, the only exophoric reference (that is, to an entity not retrievable from the text) is to the study itself ('this paper') or its producers ('we'). This tendency for largely endophoric reference is consistent with the mode of 'language-as-reflection' rather than 'language-as-action', as suggested by Ventola (1987: 148). That is, the language tracks the participants as entities in the text rather than as entities in the non-verbal world as would be the case, for example, in a news interview where the two major participants gain their identity and continuity by their physical presence.

The actual realization of the participants is largely through the phoricity system and, within phoricity, through the articles and demonstrative pronouns (e.g. 'the', 'this', 'that'). The demonstrative 'here' typically signifies the text that the reader is dealing with. The only personal pronoun commonly used is 'we', referring to the authors. Thus our analysis concentrates on endophoric reference that ties the participants in the text to each other.

The issue that arises in tracking participants is the relation between the participants and the linguistic signals that are used to track them. The initial item in reference strings tends to be generic, e.g. 'many investigators', 'several surveys', 'a topic of discussion', whereas the subsequent items in the chain tend to be specific (e.g. 'V and R, 1980', 'that study'). The majority of ties in these chains depend on an implied relationship between the first referent and its co-referent that occurs later. This relationship takes one of two forms, either:

1. one item in the chain refers to a member or component of the entity established in another item, such as 'Many investigators have found . . .' followed by 'Jones (1991) reports . . .', which refers to part of 'many investigators'; or

2. different aspects of the same item (research product and producer) are used interchangeably. In other words, the same entity in the real world can surface in the text as different participants with an implied relationship between them. Although the participants may have opposing semantic features (either [+animate] or [−animate]) there is still a relationship between the participants. For example, in the following text the names of producers ([+animate]) and the products of research ([−animate]) are used interchangeably to refer to the products.

(a) **P and W**, 1978 [producer: +animate] compare the reactions of . . .

(b) **this study** [product: −animate] involved a relatively small sample . . .

(c) like **P and W** [producer: +animate]

(d) **most of the studies in the . . . literature** . . . [product: −animate]

(e) For example, **V and R**, 1980 [producer: +animate] found that . . .

(f) **In that study** [product: −animate] (Text 8)

The above example of reference also shows the difficulty of tracking participants in the research article genre. This example could be one chain with five participants:
1. P and W, 2. their study (expressed as 'this study'), 3. most of the studies, 4. V and R, and 5. their study (expressed as 'that study'). Alternately, the example could be taken as two chains. The first chain consists of: 1. P and W, 2. this study, 3. like P and W. The second chain is: 1. most of the studies in the . . . literature, 2. V and R, 3. that study. In terms of the genre, this indeterminacy is a statement that the genre does not require a precise linking of these participants at this point in the unfolding of the text. In terms of our earlier metaphor, sometimes it does not matter if the thread is seen as navy blue or sky blue.

As well as an indeterminacy from one entity in the real world to different participants in the text (product or producer), participants in the text that have the same or similar realizations (studies, surveys) can encode different entities in the real world. For example, the fifteen items of studies–surveys–etc. in the text below (Text 3) represent eight different participants. Each non-phoric item is considered as starting a chain with the items that continue that chain listed in the same line.

1. Several surveys
2. A number of studies – these studies – the studies
3. Laboratory experiments – this setting
4. Prior studies
5. Most studies

6. Systematic prospective studies – such studies
7. Similar studies – our group – others – these inpatient studies – our study
   – these inpatient studies – our study
8. Studies – reports

In terms of the relations between items in a chain, the above example shows that the phoricity system does not necessarily differentiate between presuming and presenting items. For example, 'several surveys' (chain 1) and 'a number of studies' (chain 2) are encoded as presenting new participants. However, the content of the sentences in context suggests that 'a number of studies' may be co-referential with 'several studies'. Similarly, 'prior studies' (chain 4) and 'most studies' (chain 5) may be co-referential. Again 'studies' and 'reports' (both in chain 8) seem co-referential even though 'reports' is not specifically encoded as presuming. Despite the fact that each generic item typically starts a new chain (Martin, 1992: 146), the micro-chains in the above example are not co-extensive with the trajectory of the participants in the text. There are linguistic realizations of participants in a text, the participants themselves, and entities in the real world. Although the mapping from one level to another follows general patterns there is not a one-to-one relationship.

Another way that relations are built in a chain when there is not identity among the items in the chain is through relevance. In relevance phoricity 'the identity of one or more participants related to the participant being realized is recoverable' (Martin, 1992: 100). Therefore, in examples such as 'one of our concerns', 'another concern', an attribute or membership in a class is shared by the new participant with a participant mentioned earlier in the text.

There are other cases of a lack of one-to-one mapping between participants and their realizations. It could be thought that chains representing the authors and their products in nominal groups would refer to the same real world entities. However, this relationship is only valid for the product ('the present study', 'the study'). For producers, although the exophoric reference 'we' realizes the authors in Move 3 ('preview the authors' contribution'), some of the realizations of 'we' in Move 1 ('claim relevance') are interchangeable with 'one'. That is, 'we' is used in a general sense. For example, sometimes 'we' represents the discourse community as in 'We might expect . . .', 'if we consider life stress . . .' (Text 9). In other cases, 'we' may represent the entire culture, as in 'How do we come to categorize . . .' (Text 11).

The item 'we' enters into yet another ambiguity. 'We' can be used by the present authors to refer to a group of which they are only a part. For example, the authors Lin and Ensel state that 'We have recently presented studies . . . [Lin, Dean and Ensel] . . .' (Text 9). Precisely put, this statement would have been 'We, along with Dean, have . . .'. However, the conventions of the research article genre accept that 'we' can be used in different ways and that the potential ambiguity is acceptable. A similar example of exophoric reference expanding to include a new participant is 'We met George at the airport. Then we all went out for dinner' (Grimes, 1975: 46).

The genre of research articles presents an additional problem in the tracking of participants. As well as changing their identity or composition, sometimes participants seem to change state. Halliday and Hasan (1976: 2) note that a lexicogrammatical realization that codes for 'the same participant' can actually represent one that has undergone a change of physical state, e.g. 'Wash and core six cooking apples. Put them into a fireproof dish', for which 'them' is certainly not the same as the apples in the first sentence. In the genre of the SSR article, there is an interesting phenomenon of participants undergoing a change from uncertain to certain. Take the following example from Text 3: '. . . we are unaware of any large prospective trial of the effects of withdrawal on cessation success. *The fact* that such a study has never been published is a glaring gap in the tobacco withdrawal literature'. The hedged denial in the first sentence ('we are unaware of . . .') of a certain participant ('any large prospective trial') becomes a reality ('the fact that . . .') in the second sentence. Similarly, in Text 6, speculation ('may be signs', 'may disrupt') in the following example becomes 'evidence': '. . . reactions such as anxiety . . . may be signs of early adjustment difficulties that, in turn, may disrupt children's future progress. Given *this evidence* there is a need to identify the potential antecedents and concomitants of successful school transitions' [emphasis added].

A similar change towards stronger generalization may characterize the genre. The following excerpts from the same article compare statements of results from the Discussion sections that appear after each separate study with the general Discussion that appears at the end of the article. After the first study, it is stated that 'Newscasters 1 and 2 [two of the three studied] did not exhibit any noticeable bias . . . However, Newscaster 3 did appear to exhibit a strong positive bias in favor of Reagan'. The Discussion after the second study states that 'Although the effect for each sample is a modest one, each of the contrasts is in the predicted direction'. In the general Discussion, where the various studies are summarized, the conclusions are stronger: 'The results of Studies 1 and 2 indicate that newscasters can and do exhibit biases in facial expressions while referring to political candidates and that such biases are associated with complementary voting patterns on the part of viewers' (Text 7). The general Discussion section reflects the following changes:

1. one newscaster has been extended to the generic 'newscaster'
2. uncertainty ('appeared to') has become neutral ('newscasters can and do')
3. the qualified 'a modest effect' is generalized to 'biases are associated with . . .'.

The changes in the representation of participants reflect the interweaving of the interpersonal dimension with the discoursal structures. Whether such flexibility is characteristic of the genre itself is an important topic for future studies.

As well as considering how participants are tracked and how those participants are realized in chains of references, we must also deal with reference structures and how participant orientation is presented in the texts. Major work on the identity and expression of participants was presented by Grimes (1975). Grimes was interested in the relation between a participant's role in the discourse as a whole and the participant's semantic role in each particular action.

Discourse roles include, for example, 'the initiator' as the participant who throughout the discourse carries the action forward and a 'reactor' who is the participant affected by the action in the discourse. Semantic roles, on the other hand, identify how involved the participant is in the action and, in descending order of involvement, are: agent, former state, latter state, patient, instrument, force, benefactive, and range. Grimes showed that there is an interaction between the participant's role in the discourse as a whole and its role in particular episodes. In our terms, then, there is a construction of dependency relations through the text and these relations of overall structure are intertwined with the participant roles in more local structures.

Regarding overall text structure, Grimes proposes that there are equilibrium states among the participants in a text and various tension states as those participants play different roles in the text. For example, the story may start with an equilibrium state for which the narrator is both the teller of the story and major actor in it. The narrator consequently may start the story with a performative placing himself as teller and actor (e.g. 'I was part of the hunt for the spirit of rebellion several years ago'). In this initial equilibrium state, the teller is actor and the spirit of rebellion is patient. The story may end with another equilibrium state with the participants in the same relationship to each other: 'the place where I killed him was in that direction' ('I' teller of story = agent; 'him' = 'spirit of rebellion' = patient). In between these two states of equilibrium, the participants may have other relations to each other and other participants may be involved. These are the tension states. A text then is made up of participants who are in certain relations to each other and these relations may change as the text unfolds. Although Grimes' work was on folk stories, it is possible that research 'stories' share antecedents with oral narratives, as we suggested in Chapter 3 ('Introductions as narratives'). Grimes' work inspires the following questions:

1. Is there a correspondence between the type of participant and the generic structure? and
2. Is there a correspondence between type of participant and discourse role (such as 'initiator' or 'reactor')?

Grimes (1975) shows that for folk narratives there are systematic alternations in the semantic and thematic roles of the main participant and supporting participants. However, the data from the research texts do not support such changes in the roles of participants. The only clear change in semantic roles of participants occurs for Move 3 ('preview the authors' contribution'; see Chapter 3). In Move 1 ('claim relevance') and Move 2 ('establish the gap'), the authors play either no role or a minor role, referring to themselves in the third person ('Jones 1990 reports . . .'). However, in Move 3, the authors, often realized by a pronoun, 'we', become prominent. Moreover, in Move 3, the authors tend to assume the role of reporter, e.g. 'we present', 'we report', or initiator of research activity: 'we posed three questions', 'we chose', 'we decided to use'.

A more general question inspired by Grimes (1975) is whether there is an academic equivalent of 'once upon a time . . . and they lived happily ever after'.

In narratives, there is an equilibrium state that starts and ends a narrative along with various states of tension in which the characters change their roles until the equilibrium state is re-established at the end of the story. The narrative is then a series of shifts in the roles that the participants take. Perhaps the claim of relevance (Move 1) is equivalent to the equilibrium state, since the accepted facts of the research community are asserted, e.g. 'Major changes in work and leisure activities . . . have occurred in the US in the last few decades' (Text 2). The equilibrium state introduces minor characters as the participants, namely, other researchers. The major activities are introduced in Move 3 ('preview the authors' contribution') with the authors taking over the role of major participant and with the introduction of the substantive participants of the research topic. This juncture between equilibrium state and the new state of tension that will ultimately be resolved is often marked by the foregrounding by thematization of the new major participant, often 'we', e.g. 'We report here the results of three studies . . .' (Text 5).

The analogy to a narrative can be extended into the Discussion section. The end of a research article is usually realized by Move E, 'state implications', e.g. '[X] remains a question for further research' (Text 2). Having triumphed over one set of obstacles, the narrator then suggests a new tension state with a new uncertainty to resolve: '. . . whether social trends that improve the quality of life for some groups also produce a greater risk of victimization among these individuals remains a question for further research' (Text 2). This new tension state is then the equilibrium state for the next narrative of scientific research on the topic.

So far, all our analyses have been of the 'research narrative', which we have shown to be quite dynamic, as it responds to rhetorical needs. It is possible that the tracking system for more static entities, i.e. the phenomena being investigated, will be less flexible. In order to compare the reference system dealing with the phenomena to that dealing with the research narrative, one type of participant was analysed in eight Introduction sections. The participant common to all the texts (since the articles were from the social sciences) is the group of human beings being studied. The lists of nominal groups do not necessarily constitute strings tracking the same participants. Texts have various methods of referring to this participant. The subjects of a study are referred to variously (1) by their membership in the class 'human beings' (*individuals*, *men and women*, *persons*, *infants* or *children*, Texts 1, 2, 5, 6); (2) by their membership in the class 'subjects of inquiry' (*respondents*, *subjects*, Text 8); or (3) by their membership in the class 'people who embody the variables of the study' (*smokers*, Text 3). The texts sometimes refer to these participants by membership in one of the above groups or by membership in two of the groups.

The findings show that the tracking system for research phenomena is more rigid and uniform than that for research narratives. When referring to the human subjects of the social science research, ambiguous forms are avoided so that pronouns are exceedingly rare. Rather than referring to 'the first group' or 'the second group', or substituting 'they', the authors spell out the variables each time the participant is mentioned (e.g. 'television viewers who watch the newscasters on a regular basis', Text 7). Similarly, synonyms are avoided; hence, multiple references to the research subject use the same term: 'infants' and not 'babies' (Text 5), 'children' rather than 'pupils' or 'students' (although the children were studied in a school setting) (Text 6). Thus, there are indications that participants that are part of the narrative line may be tracked differently from those that are related to the phenomena being described.

Summary

The major differences between the narrative genres described in other studies and scientific texts is that narratives typically centre around a few participants that traverse the text and interact with each other (e.g. Grimes, 1975; Martin, 1992) while research texts present many participants that traverse relatively short portions of the text and retain separate identities. The range of participants reflects the fact that in reviewing literature the author is telling not one story but a number of stories each with its own 'heroes'.

The participant identification system in research texts is sensitive to generic structure in very basic ways. Rather than an animate entity, the most frequently realized participant in the Introductions is 'past research', while the most frequently realized participant in the Discussions is 'present research'. This distribution of course conforms to the emphasis of each of these two sections of research articles. Similarly, the participant 'present research' emerges in Move 3 ('preview the authors' contribution'), while the participant 'problems' emerges in Move 2 ('establish the gap') and in Move D ('ward off counterclaims'). The authors, hitherto narrators, emerge as actors as well in Move 3, 'preview the authors' contribution'. In addition to the role of the narrator/actor, there seem to be some parallels to the equilibrium–tension states identified in folk tales by Grimes (1975).

Our principal finding is that participant identification is a much more complicated issue for research texts than for the oral and/or narrative genres reported in the literature. Several problems appear in the participant tracking system used in these SSR texts. Boundaries between different entities are ambiguous. Ties between realizations of the same referent are based upon implied rather than direct or explicit relationships. Possibly, the trajectory of participants in 'past research' is meant to be traced through the citation system rather than through the linguistic reference system. Alternatively, participant identification systems in the research narrative have a very small role to play in research texts, as befits a genre in which human intervention, at least, is to be downplayed. There are indications that participants that form the phenomenological field account for a greater proportion of reference items than do entities in the research narrative strand. In addition, it is possible that in this genre, textual unity depends less upon 'active' participants and more upon the lexical cohesion system and the form of the research narrative (chronological ordering, progression from general to specific phenomena, and the very basic problem/solution discourse pattern, as discussed in Chapters 1 and 3).

We have raised an additional issue that could be relevant to the question of the social construction of scientific knowledge. These are examples in which the second reference to a claim undergoes a change of state from certain to uncertain or from a weaker to a stronger generalization. Further analysis of a larger number of texts is needed to verify this issue.

The current study also highlights problematic issues in existing methods for the analysis of participant tracking systems. For example, the approaches of Halliday and Hasan (1976), Ventola (1987) and Martin (1992) unite items tied by comparative or other relevance structures. Thus, these items have different referents by definition. Furthermore, generic nominal groups that realize identical participants must be assigned to different chains since chains are formulated on the basis of phoricity. A system that would follow the progress of participants, rather than merely identify them, awaits development.

7   Signalling beginnings and endings

Introduction

As we have outlined in previous chapters, one of the purposes of the present work is to provide a complete characterization of the generic variety of Introduction and Discussion sections of research articles in social science journals. We have provided, in Chapter 2, a method for determining units of analysis and their realizations so that future analyses of the genre of research texts could be related to a common working model. Chapters 3 and 4 delineate the rhetorical structures (elements defined by their communicative purposes) that characterize this genre. Further steps towards a thorough characterization were taken in Chapter 5, where we examined the role of lexical cohesion; Chapter 6 focused on the role of participants. To complete the characterization of generic structures, we turn now to the last element, that of the boundary marking system, beginning with definitions of relevant terms. We then briefly discuss related work on boundaries and genre, after which we focus on the specific findings of this study.

Definitions

Boundaries

A boundary is the juncture at which two different linguistic or discourse elements meet. In some texts, boundaries are not marked by conventional signals, while in others junctures are explicitly indicated by conventional signals.

Perhaps the most familiar set of signals to mark openings and closings of linguistic structures is punctuation, in which full stops mark sentence boundaries, and commas mark boundaries between nominal groups. Equally familiar are boundaries between ideational units, marked by, for example, conjunctive elements such as *next, first, second, moreover*, which establish cohesion between stretches of discourse as well as organize the discourse into sub-ideas, evident in: 'The additive burden hypothesis ... also considers situation and personal characteristics ...'; 'The *next* hypothesis, the chronic burden hypothesis ... posits that ...' (Text 9) [emphasis added].

Boundaries can also be signalled paralinguistically, for example, in casual conversation by pauses and in written texts by the use of special fonts.

To begin with, we will distinguish between boundary signals (or markers) and boundary frames. The features of a frame must be independent of the features of the act it is framing; this difference is illustrated in the following quotations from Text 7:

1. The results of Studies 1 and 2 indicate that [x relationship was found].
2. The results of Study 1 can be summarized as follows.

Example (1) is a boundary signal but not a frame because it realizes the act 'reporting accomplishments', which we have shown above (Figures 4.5 and 4.6) must contain a reference to the authors and a claim about their findings. Example (2) is a boundary frame because it is does not carry features of the realization of the act itself.

The literature on scientific research texts refers to *signals* of moves (Swales, 1990; Dudley-Evans, 1994) that are an integral part of the realization of the move itself. To Dudley-Evans, lexical items such as *an examination* or *revealed* clearly indicate a finding.

A prototype of a boundary frame in an oral genre is provided by Sinclair and Coulthard's study of school lessons (1975: 63):

Teacher: Finished?
Pupil: Yes.
Boundary: Teacher: *Right.*
Teacher: Read us what you've written, Joan.

In this instance, *Right* marks the boundary between two tasks within a lesson. In another example of instructional discourse, Grosz (1975/82) finds similar boundary markers between sub-tasks, e.g. 'Now the next thing you do . . . OK (and) What should I do now?'

Conjunctions are one device for producing cohesion within a text as they encode logical relations between units of text. They may also function as realizations of boundary frames. The complexity of meanings encoded by conjunctions is shown for one class, concessives, in Figure 7.1.

The choice of type of conjunction, of course, reflects mode, which is particularly evident in the differential distribution in oral and written modes, e.g. of *and* and *but* in the former, and of *moreover* and *nevertheless* in the latter. Although Halliday and Hasan (1976) and Martin (1983) consider terms such as *well* and *anyway* as conjunctions, these terms should be classified differently from those that encode logical relations, since *well* and *anyway* are semantically empty, serving also as pause fillers, and, in clause-initial position as boundary markers. Those conjunctions that have been found to frame discourse elements (Sinclair and Coulthard, 1975; Ventola, 1987; Martin, 1983) are of the semantically empty type.

Markers, like conjunctions, may be genre-specific; in narratives, different units are distinguishable ('partitioned') by markers that indicate change of setting (time or place) and theme (the person or thing talked about) (Grimes, 1975). On

Figure 7.1 Conjunction in English, highlighting system network for concessives

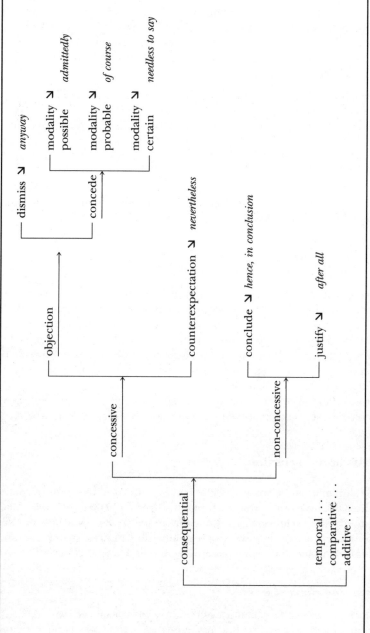

Adapted from Martin, 1983: 3; 1992: 224, used with permission of John Benjamins Publishing Co.
The items in italics are examples of realizations.

the other hand, time and place are irrelevant in presenting a philosophical argument where changes in the direction of the argument figure significantly, as in the following:

> para. 1: Other questions have sometimes been asked . . .
> para. 2: Another question sometimes asked is this . . .
> para. 3: The only correct answer is the straightforward one . . .
> para. 4: It has also been said that the problem of induction is . . . (Popper, 1963: 56).

It is reasonable to expect that, as well as demarcating linguistic structures and idea units, boundary frames might operate to distinguish elements of generic structure (which, in the present corpus, are moves and acts). As Martin (1983: 56) suggests: 'Certain internal conjunctions, *now*, *okay*, *anyway* and *by the way*, for example, have as their sole function demarcating stages, or elements of schematic structure, in a text'.

For example, in the following text, *so* is used to mark the *Set Ground* and *State Problem* elements of schematic structure in an advertisement genre with the functional tenor of persuasion:

> Lips are a must.
> They're in fashion.
> *So* what are you using in your skin care?

The few studies that have focused on framing found that genres vary in the degree to which their internal structures are framed, with instructional discourse characterized by framing to a high degree (Sinclair and Coulthard, 1975), and service encounters so characterized to a minimal degree (Ventola, 1987). Moreover, the *type* of boundary frame realized may be genre-sensitive; *well*, *right*, *now* and *okay* are among those terms characteristic of activity-oriented oral discourse, e.g. lessons (Sinclair and Coulthard, 1975) and service encounters (Ventola, 1987). Temporal conjunctions are prominent in narratives, in which chronological sequencing of events is important (Brown and Yule, 1983).

Results and discussion

After examining the opening and closing elements of all moves in Introductions and Discussions in the present corpus, we found that no structure functions consistently and exclusively as a frame for any move as does 'Right' or 'Now' in school lessons. However, we can examine the devices that mark opening boundaries in some moves; no patterns were found among closures.

Formatting conventions

Fifty per cent of opening boundaries of moves are coextensive with the initiation of orthographic paragraphs. But in some cases, paragraphs contain more than one move, while in others, a move extends beyond one paragraph.

Although subtitles framing Methods, Results and Discussion are common to all texts, in only one section of one text (an Introduction) do the subtitles function to delineate moves. More often, when subtitles are provided, their function is to organize the discourse according to idea units rather than rhetorical functions, e.g.

Predicting Children's Social Competence
Predicting Children's School Adjustment (Text 6)

Subtitles actually frame moves in only one text:

Problems with Previous Tests
Hypotheses (Text 2)

Lexicogrammatical structures

Conjunctions

Conjunctions as a class do not signal move boundaries in the present corpus but one type, concessive, tends to signal the act of pointing out gaps in research. Concessives 'signal the unexpected, surprising nature of what is being said in view of what was said before that' (Quirk *et al.*, 1991: 674).

The present texts rely heavily on *although, while, however* and *nonetheless*; they are the only concessives realized in Introductions and the predominant ones in Discussions. Of the conjunctions of concession realized, *although* and *however* are preferred. The preference in our corpus of SSR texts for these two conjunctions as a subordinator and non-subordinator, respectively, may be due to some feature in those particular items. For instance, Martin (1983) claims 'although' and 'even though' both select the same features in the hierarchy of delicacy (reading from left to right): external: relation effected: nonpurposive: cause: cause subordinate: concessive. But at the highest level of delicacy, *although* selects 'approval unmarked' compared to *even though* which selects for 'disapproval'. Similarly, among markers of contrast, *while* and *whereas* select the feature 'expectation unmarked' compared to *instead* which carries the feature 'subordinate unexpected'. Martin does not provide the features for *however* and the other concessives realized in the present study but his remarks about *although* and *while* suggest that in scientific writing conjunctions are chosen for 'unmarkedness', i.e. the most neutral option in a particular class is chosen. As with lexical items (Chapter 5), the author selects from the appropriate register those conjunctions consonant with his/her interpersonal purposes. The choice of a subordinator versus non-subordinator may also be author-specific. Nine out of eleven concessive conjunctions in Text 8 are subordinators, while seven out of eight of the concessive conjunctions in Text 12 are non-subordinators.[1]

When all pairs of clauses in Introductions that are joined by concessive conjunctions are considered, 26 out of 36 of these conjunctions signal 'surprise' (a term used by Quirk *et al.*, 1991) at a potential deficiency in research or its interpretation (as in [A] in the following text). Only three conjunctions signal surprise at a discrepancy in the phenomenon being discussed (as in [B] in the following text) [concessives underlined]:

(B) The majority of respondents showed improvement from the first to second interview, <u>although</u> a sizable minority (27 per cent to 37 per cent) continued to experience a variety of symptoms . . . (A) <u>Nonetheless</u>, the authors [N, N and N] concluded from their data that bereavement is a relatively mild reaction for most subjects. A thorough review of the research in this area, <u>however</u>, does not substantiate this view of the grieving process. (Text 8)

One conjunction in our corpus signals that, in fact, a gap has been eliminated. This distribution suggests that 'surprise' (in the form of concessives) operates primarily at the interpersonal level, where the authors are evaluating their work or that of others, rather than at the experiential level.

When only initial acts of Move 2 ('establish the gap') are considered, eight out of twelve are signalled by concessives.

In addition to concessives, consequential conjunctions were analysed; it was found that consequential conjunctions do not signal any particular move or act but rather signal the end of a chain of reasoning, involving statements of fact as well as of claims. However, consequential conjunctions are used very sparingly, modifying fewer than five per cent of the independent clauses in Discussion sections (Chapter 4).

Attitudinal disjuncts

Only Move 2 ('establish the gap') can select an attitudinal disjunct. An attitudinal disjunct marks the opening of a Move 2 in only one text, i.e. 'Unfortunately, past studies provide little information about . . .' (Text 8). Since this option is so rarely exercised, attitudinal disjuncts cannot serve as a boundary signal for Move 2.

Metadiscoursal comments

Comments that announce the content of the subsequent text, but do not discuss those contents, comprise the only lexicogrammatical structure that functions exclusively as a frame. Example (3) (following) qualifies as a boundary frame, since it refers in general to 'questions' without adding any information pertinent to this study. Such a frame could be used at the appropriate juncture in any text in this genre.

(3) 'In addition to addressing these issues, the present study also examines several fundamental questions that have been neglected in previous applica- tions' (Text 2).

Introductions: If we consider as frames only those metadiscoursal comments that do not include the parameters of the contents of the study within the comment, then the comments for eight out of twelve instances of Move 3 qualify as boundary frames. It can be argued that these frames mark the boundary between Move 2 and the remainder of the paper, rather than the boundary between Moves 2 and 3. That is, the demarcation at this point seems to suffice for the remainder of the paper.

Discussions: The boundaries of only ten of 49 realized moves in Discussion sections are framed by a metadiscoursal comment, as in the following examples:

(4) 'The results of Study 1 can be summarized as follows' (Text 7, 'report accomplishments'). (5) 'Our findings, although preliminary, suggest some possible sex-related differences in the natural history of cocaine abuse' (Text 10, 'offer interpretation'). (6) 'There are several possible explanations for the poorer performance of [x] variables in explaining [y]' (Text 2, 'ward off counterclaims').

Markers other than frames

Even though boundaries are not consistently demarcated by frames, certain other conventions differentiate some boundaries.

Position

The opening boundaries of Move 1 ('claim relevance') and Move A ('report accomplishments') are established by their position (in most cases) as the first element of the Introduction and Discussion, respectively. While there is no boundary frame for these specific moves, in a general way, the title of the article serves as boundary frame for Move 1, while the subtitle *Discussion* serves as the boundary frame for Move A.

Modality

In Discussion sections, the juncture between Moves A ('report accomplishments'), and B ('evaluate congruence'), if realized, and the next element, C or D ('offer an interpretation' or 'ward off counterclaims') is marked in six out of twelve texts by a change in modality. Moves A and B do not select modality (e.g. *one result is . . ., this result is consistent with . . .*) while the subsequent move, whether C or D, selects modality, e.g.:

[MOVE A] However . . . the absence of social resources will exacerbate its negative impact on physical symptoms.
[MOVE C] The present study suggests that the life stress process is a complex one . . . (Text 9).

Lexical signals

As Chapter 3 has shown, the selection of a deictic marker and a reference to the present research product signals Move 3 ('preview authors' contribution').

However, these structures are features of the realization of Move 3, and thus do not constitute a boundary frame.

Tense

Each move has several optional pre-head acts that select independently for tense. The only tense restrictions are on the head act, e.g. *state results* cannot select futurity and *state implications* cannot select past tense. Since different realizations of each type of move can select different optional pre-head acts, changes in tense do not serve as a recognition feature for a move boundary.

Theme

For similar reasons, changes in theme (i.e. the first element in each sentence) do not serve as a recognition feature for a move boundary.

Summary

Boundary marking of idea units is a recognized feature of scholarly writing (e.g. *first, next, furthermore*). However, the question of boundary marking of generic structures, particularly in the research genre, has not been explored to date. We have begun to do so in this chapter and one of the interesting findings in our analysis is the small proportion of rhetorical functions delineated by grahic boundaries, such as paragraph initiations and subtitles. Of the boundaries that are signalled linguistically, only a small proportion are indicated by frames, i.e. structures realized independently of the move itself, such as 'The results of Study 1 can be summarized as follows'. Furthermore, transitions between moves are not typically marked by conjunctions, either of one class or a combination of classes. Because of these difficulties, determining the extent of a move poses problems. In the absence of formal boundaries, an intricate system defining the head act by realizations and adjacent acts by implicit or explicit logical connectors had to be worked out (Chapter 2).

We have to assume that the expert reader relies on knowledge of the field to recognize boundaries. Perhaps the use of 'reader-friendly' devices, such as subtitles, is a feature of expert-to-layperson or more popular texts. It may also be true that structure boundaries are primarily important in spoken inter-changes, in which turns must be allocated, while in the written mode, it is idea units that require processing and are therefore demarcated.

Furthermore, as we indicated, when boundary markers do occur, they are not of a uniform system. Instead, each type of move is associated with a specific type of signal. In the Introduction section, Move 1 ('claim relevance') is signalled by its position as first move (in ten out of twelve texts), and Move 2 ('establish the gap') is signalled in eight out of twelve texts by a concessive conjunction. Among these, the predominant choice is *however*, which may reflect the most hedged or non-judgemental option. The initiation of Move 3 ('preview the authors' contribution') is marked by a deictic and a reference to the present research product. The only type of frame for moves in the Discussion section (ten out of 49) is a metadiscoursal comment, which previews the contents of the subsequent text in that move. So while we have begun to examine the issue of boundary marking, a comparison of boundary markers in related genres is required to clarify the role of such marking in scholarly writing.

Note

1. Observations of Finnish writers of English scientific articles (Ventola and Mauranen, 1991) lead the authors to conclude that the tendency to use certain connectors rather than others is characteristic of non-native writers. They cite particularly the 'overuse' of *however* for signifying adversative [i.e. concessive] relations. However, in view of our findings, it could just as well be that these otherwise naive writers have internalized the appropriate conjunction for this scientific article genre.

8　Conclusions

Genre analysis

We set out in this study with two goals in mind, first, to contribute to a model for the characterization of genre in expository texts, showing the interweaving of generic, registerial, and discoursal options, and second, to provide a characterization of social science research (SSR) texts in particular, an academic domain that has been neglected in genre studies. We will discuss our findings and conclusions in reverse order, starting with the systems of the SSR genre and how they interact. In analysing this genre, we have suggested a rigorous system for generating realizations of each move. Previous work on research articles focused on one system, the genre structures, and did not share a consistent methodology for identifying moves. The result was widely varied types and numbers of structures in different research studies. In our attempt to arrive at a consistent, objective method, we identified generic structures according to the discourse units (moves) that convey communicative intent, rather than according to structural units such as the clause or sentence, or other lexicogrammatical criteria. In order to arrive at an objective classification of moves, we stipulated semantic criteria for their realizations, which we hope can serve for genre analysis across disciplines.

We determined prototypical elements (moves) for Introductions and Discussions, indicated the prototypical sequencing of the elements, and specified the systems that demarcate boundaries between these elements. To analyse register, we classified lexical choices. On the discourse plane, we specified lexical cohesion chains, and reference systems that enable participant identification. These last two systems help create a cohesive text from the various genre structures.

Following are the moves we identified in the Introduction and Discussion sections. Furthermore, we review how the dictates of the genre (the basic prototypical structures) become embellished with more personal rhetorical agendas of the author.

Moves in Introductions

In Move 1, 'claim relevance of field', the authors justify their choice of phenomena for intensive study; authors intensify the relevance of the present research by stressing its application to human behaviour and to as large a phenomenological field as possible, as well as its immediacy by placing the move within the frame of recent time.

In Move 2, 'establish the gap the present research is meant to fill', the authors point out that the knowledge about the phenomena that they have chosen is incomplete; while most authors motivate their research by pointing out defects in existing literature, they seem to choose semantic options that will not be face-threatening. In Move 3, 'preview the authors' contribution', the authors declare that they have carried out an investigation into the specific relevant variables. The most salient interpersonal component of Move 3 is its explicit or implicit promise to fill the gap, or to conform to an ideal research design.

Moves in Discussions

In the head act of Move A, 'report accomplishments', the authors express in more general terms the quantitative relationships between variables they have found in the present study (which have been previously reported under the Results section).

After basically repeating their results, the authors apply some qualitative yardstick to them. They usually assess their study by showing the conformity (or more typically, superiority) of their methods or results to the hypotheses, methods or results of other studies, or to general criteria for research. We have termed this Move B, 'evaluate congruence of findings with other criteria'. Move B is treated as a separate move, rather than an act supporting Move A, 'accomplishments', because Move B can appear independently of Move A.

After measuring the aptness of the present research, an explanation is called for. In the key act of Move C, the authors offer a hypothesis, which we define here as a claim, endorsed by the authors, suggesting why or how the phenomena under study are or should be related. But the authors recognize that others may see defects in their methods or posit different explanations for the results. Therefore, in the next move, D, the authors ward off counterclaims. This move, unlike the others, has two obligatory elements: *raise potential counterclaims* and *respond to the counterclaims*. Counterclaims include the possibility of deficiencies in the present methods or interpretations other than the authors'. Responding can be accomplished by either (a) accepting responsibility or by (b) dismissing counterclaims. While there is only one way to accept responsibility, dismissing counterclaims can be accomplished by a range of options, with different degrees of personal involvement.

A text could be considered complete at this point but most authors prefer to discuss the implications of their study for the future (Move E). The scale of options for the head act ranges from a very modest call for continued research on the variables under study to a more assertive recommendation for a change in the theoretical stance of the discipline or in social policy to reflect the results of the study.

In addition to the basic moves, we examined two acts (which fill slots in moves). We found that authors offer personal opinions (stating comments), albeit rarely. Equally surprisingly, authors largely abstain from stating conclusions or, to put it more precisely, they abstain from signalling conclusions as such; furthermore, acts that are signalled as conclusions frequently co-occur with a structure of uncertainty, thereby neutralizing the definiteness of the conclusion. This failure to 'conclude' decisively may be a function of the need to dilute new claims so that impositions are not made upon the reader, another reflection of politeness strategies (Brown and Levinson, 1987).

Although Introduction and Discussion sections are comprised of prototypical moves, these moves are not rigid. From all the moves associated with the genre, the author has discretion to omit two or three. This is because the constraints of the genre interact with certain elements of the context/situation (e.g. whether the results of the research were satisfactory to the authors). As these choices are made, they constrain subsequent choices of structures. We have adapted Ventola's (1987) flowchart method to account for the flexibility of structures in Discussion texts.

Authors can decide not only which of the prototypical moves to realize (beyond a certain minimum) but also how much to highlight each move, i.e. the proportion of text to devote to each move. In addition, the order can be manipulated and moves can be realized in composite or in cyclical form.

Characterizing expository text by genre, first of all, means determining the customary discourse structures (moves and their constituent acts); these in turn are defined by their communicative purposes. The notion of 'genre' presupposes a set of socially prescribed events; we say a text belongs to a genre because it encapsulates most of the structures we have come to expect from that genre. This would seem to presuppose a set of outcomes, as in the Hollywood genres of Western, murder mystery and so on. However, we have tried to present evidence for the claim that generic structures either evolve from or are shaped by interpersonal needs. Within particular generic structures, we see ongoing conflicts between the scientist as neutral observer and as emotionally involved participant, and between the author as narrator of the tale and as protagonist.

But a text is not shaped by genre structure alone, although it may be the system that drives the other systems. While the moves create the horizontal structuring in a text, with each move accounting for a segment of the text, the vertical discourse elements of lexical cohesion and reference weave the generic structures into a unified text. In other words, a text may realize the generic structures and still be disjointed. Lexical cohesion and the reference to participants that traverse the text create textual unity.

Lexical cohesion

Our analysis of lexical cohesion of the research strand in eight SSR texts shows that this genre has characteristic lexical features. There are three reasons for this conclusion. First, the lexical ties in the chains are almost always based on repetition and synonymy. This concentration on these two types of lexical tie reflects the fact that scientific texts tend to use resources aimed at clarity and definition, in contrast to non-scientific, oral and/or narrative texts. Second, the lexical choices in these chains belong to a limited set of eight semantic categories. Third, the lexical chains in the various texts draw their realizations from a small selection of the total options available.

Beyond this basic lexical unity, the lexical register for SSR texts undergoes successive screenings, which select options in accordance with social expectations and personal rhetorical aims. Such fine tuning suggests that the boundaries of field, mode and tenor are not clear-cut. It is possible that choices, such as hedging structures, which originally reflected selections of tenor (e.g. politeness, modesty) have been institutionalized in the choices that now help form the mode values in research journal articles.

In the traditional view, field, mode and tenor are seen as independent factors. In this view, a phrase such as 'the data suggest' would be controlled by field (research), 'this paper' by mode (journal article), and 'we' and 'other researchers' largely by tenor. However, the view we espouse sees these choices as representing the confluence of the three streams of input. Replacing 'we' with 'the data' as the agent of 'suggest' creates empiricist discourse, which presents reality as independent of human perception and hides the authors as the interpreters of fact. The use of the process 'suggest' encodes the features of non-contention and modest conviction about the truth value of the proposition. Thus, social relationships impinge upon choices of field. In fact, the resulting configuration of choices then become identified with certain institutionalized forms of communication, leaving a lasting imprint upon the mode.

Reference

The major differences between the narrative genres described in other studies and scientific texts is that narratives typically centre around a few participants, mostly animate, which traverse the text and interact with one other (e.g. Grimes, 1975; Martin, 1992), while research texts present many participants, mostly inanimate, which traverse relatively short portions of the text and retain separate identities, reflecting the fact that the review of literature encompasses a number of stories, each with its own 'heroes'. On the other hand, although the tracking systems may be different in scientific texts, there are some vestiges of narratives, which we will discuss later.

The participant identification system in research texts is sensitive to generic structure only in very basic ways. The most frequently realized participants are 'past research' and 'present research' in Introductions and Discussions respectively, conforming to the emphasis of each of these two sections. Similarly, on the level of moves, the dominant participant is consistent with the function of the move.

Our principal finding is that participant identification is a much more complicated issue for research texts than for the oral and/or narrative genres reported in the literature. Several problems appear in the participant tracking system used in these SSR texts. Boundaries between different entities are ambiguous. Ties between realizations of the same referent are based upon implied rather than direct or explicit relationships, e.g. different aspects of the same participant are used interchangeably, such as 'Jones' research' and 'Jones'. Participant identification systems in the narrative strand of the texts have a very small role to play, as befits a genre in which human intervention is at least to be downplayed. There are indications that the dominant reference system is composed of participants that form the phenomenological field, i.e. the variables being studied. In addition, it is also possible that in this genre, textual unity is achieved mostly by the lexical cohesion system and other elements of organization, such as chronological ordering, progression from general to specific ideas, and the very basic research/problem–solution discourse frame.

We have raised an additional issue that could be relevant to the question of the social construction of scientific knowledge. There are examples in which the second reference to a claim undergoes a change of state from certain to uncertain or from a weaker to a stronger generalization. Further analysis of a larger number of texts is needed to verify this issue.

Boundary marking

While the reference system involves considerable ambiguities, the boundary marking system is almost nonexistent. Only a small proportion of rhetorical functions are delineated by formal boundaries, whether linguistic, such as conjunctions, or graphic, such as paragraph initiations and subtitles. Furthermore, when boundary markers do occur, they are not uniform, but specific to the move. For instance, Move 2, 'establish the gap', is usually signalled by a concessive conjunction. The initiation of Move 3, 'preview the authors' contribution', is marked by a reference to the present research product.

Even fewer of these functions are bounded by frames, that is, structures realized independently of the move itself, such as metadiscoursal comments as in 'The results of Study 1 can be summarized as follows'. In the absence of explicit boundaries, we defined the head act by realization criteria and adjacent acts by their implicit or explicit logical connections to the head act.

Since transitions between moves were so sporadically signalled, we have to assume that the expert reader relies on knowledge of the field to recognize boundaries. Perhaps the use of 'reader-friendly' devices, such as subtitles, is a feature of expert-to-layperson or more popular texts. It may also be true that boundaries of discourse units such as moves are primarily important in spoken interchanges, in which turns must be allocated, while in the written mode, it is units based on ideational content that are demarcated.

General conclusions

The specific findings we have outlined for SSR texts lead us to two generalizations, both of which may refute any lingering stereotypes about scientific writing. First, a research article is not the antithesis of a narrative text, and second, the didactic function does not overrule the persuasive function. Perhaps the lines between text types have to be redrawn.

Table 8.1   Comparison of types of text structures

Oral narratives	**Problem/solution	Research texts
setting *[equilibrium]	situation	INTRODUCTION relevance (Move 1)
complication *[tension]	aspect of situation requiring a response	gap (Move 2)
coda resolution	response to aspect of situation requiring a response	announcement that resolution will follow (Move 3) METHODS
	result of response to aspect of situation requiring a response	RESULTS
evaluation *[equilibrium]	evaluation of result of response	DISCUSSION evaluate (Move B)
exhortation		recommendations for future (Move E)

Key: * Grimes, 1975; ** Hoey, 1983

In Chapter 1, we presented a continuum of text types evolving from oral narratives in preliterate societies to the problem/solution structure described by Hoey (1983). The research paper can be considered as the next point on the continuum both historically and in terms of rhetorical complexity. We have tried to schematize this continuum in Table 8.1.

Certain elements in the SSR texts can be seen as analogous to narrative structures:

SETTING: As setting orients the reader in physical space and time, relevance orients the reader in intellectual space by positing a question that has not been answered (as in [a] below) or a social problem that has not been solved, or a timeless and universal phenomenon (as in [b] below):

(a) 'How do we come to categorize ourselves as a member of one sex or the other?' (Text 11)

(b) 'When people are induced to act happy, they feel happier' (Text 12).

COMPLICATION: This introduces a problematic state, as does Move 2, 'establish the gap', in research texts, e.g. 'A final concern with studies on tobacco withdrawal is that several important facets of the disorder have not been well described' (Text 3).

RESOLUTION: In research texts, this element begins with an announcement that resolution will follow, i.e. Move 3, 'preview the authors' contribution': 'The present study provides a detailed and systematic description of tobacco withdrawal so that many of these unanswered questions can be addressed' (Text 3).

The other components of the Resolution are:

Method: 'Subjects were tested for tolerance to nicotine by . . .' (Text 3);
Results (presented in quantitative form) and Discussion, which, at minimum, repeats the results, but sometimes announces that the Complication has been resolved, as in 'In summary, the present study clarified several aspects of tobacco withdrawal . . .' (Text 3).
EVALUATION: This element is analogous to Move B, 'evaluate congruence of findings to other criteria', e.g. 'Two findings suggest the tobacco withdrawal syndrome possesses both interrater and intrarater reliability' (Text 3).
EXHORTATION: This element is reflected in Move E, 'state implications for research' or, as in the following example, for the real world: 'As children undertake the transition to kindergarten, it may be helpful to engineer as much continuity as possible . . .' (Text 6).

Having triumphed over one set of obstacles, the narrator then suggests a new tension state with a new uncertainty to resolve: '. . . whether social trends that improve the quality of life for some groups also produce a greater risk of victimization among these individuals remains a question for further research' (Text 2). This new tension state is then the equilibrium state for the next narrative of scientific research on the topic.

The parallels have been commented upon previously by others. Grimes (1975) likens scientific discourse to the narrative, specifically the folk tale, even though many or all of the participants in the former may be abstractions. Similarly, Dubois (1992) concludes that the article-as-story/narrative can easily be fitted into the formula for a fairy tale. The point is elegantly made by Richardson:

> When we write science, whether we recognize it or not, we write a narrative and create some kind of narrative meaning . . . the narrative mode is contextually embedded and looks for particular connections between events [which give it the meaning]. Whenever we write science, we are telling some kind of story, or some part of a larger narrative . . . we are, at the very least, embedding our research in a metanarrative, about, for example, how science progresses or how art is accomplished (Lyotard, 1979). Even the shape of the conventional research report reveals a narratively driven subtext: theory (literature review) is the past (or the researcher's) cause for the present study (the hypothesis being tested), which will lead to the future – findings and implications (for the researcher, the researched, and science) . . . Scientists often resist recognizing that their writings are particular kinds of narratives and that their writing practices are value constituting. Rather, they seem to be easily 'duped' by their own writing practices, which suppress how real people (the researchers) are ordering and constituting reality, because they draw upon the logico-scientific code (Bruner, 1986), which represents itself as objective and true. (Richardson, 1990: 13)

While we do not suggest that all science texts are narratives, SSR texts clearly retain narrative elements. This leads to the conclusion that genres have to be described in terms of constituent structures rather than broad categories such as narrative vs. expository, persuasive vs. didactic or objective.

In addition, the myth of scientific objectivity, which has been questioned by others, in our study is brought to light by the role of tenor in SSR texts. The stance in scientific discourse is usually seen as objective (non-persuasive) and the relationship between writer and reader as impersonal. The use of passive constructions and hedging structures in scientific discourse, for example, has traditionally served to obscure its persuasive aspects. Attention has been given to hedging but not to the occurrence of direct (non-hedged) claims, e.g. 'This argument is also untenable because . . .' (Text 7). We do not know which proportion of claims are hedged, which are direct (lack a hedging structure), or at the other extreme, which include a boast, e.g. 'The present finding that social resources serve as buffering force for physical health fills an obvious gap in the literature . . .' (Text 9). Our study has demonstrated that only certain types of claims (offering interpretations or raising counterclaims) tend to be hedged. We have also pointed out persuasive features of certain types of claims regardless of whether they are hedged.

Interpersonal elements are woven into the text in other ways. Although SSR texts are devoted to observations about empirical data, the text in which these intentions are embedded consists of a regulating of relations with peers. Social scientists can praise others, as in 'In a path-breaking set of papers . . .' (Text 1) or themselves, e.g. 'We believe the validity of our results is greater than that of prior studies for several reasons' (Text 3). Scientists can openly reveal their feelings: '. . . we are encouraged by the viability and meaningfulness of the results' (Text 9).

Albeit obliquely, they can also admit to being caught by surprise: 'Although the results fit the general expectations quite nicely, they were more complex than anticipated' (Text 12). Although exercising a great deal of caution, authors can criticize others, as in 'Why he reached this conclusion is somewhat unclear . . .' (Text 12) and less often, themselves: 'The lack of predictive findings . . . may be due to our failure to evaluate how . . .' (Text 1).

When faced with potential counterclaims, authors can try to mitigate their own culpability by weakening the counterclaims (through projection and modality), as in 'One could try to make the case that . . .' (Text 7) or by blaming the variables, as in 'In their present form, routine activities . . . theories are basically unfalsifiable since . . .' (Text 2).

Scientists can be rather assertive in directing the behaviour of the reader, e.g. 'This linkage should not be overlooked or disdained merely because of the low level of the relationship' (Text 4). Finally, the author, as main actor, can promise to slay the next dragon in the tale: 'The next logical step would be . . . We are currently engaged in such a program of investigation' (Text 9).

Some of these strategies represent an attempt to be polite, modest and objective, while others reflect the contrasting need to show one's own conclusions in the best possible light. The ensuing text can be seen as an attempt to resolve the constant tension between these two sets of needs.

The rhetorical structure of these SSR texts itself (rather than particular variations) furthers the persuasive function in a more general sense. The present structure of the Introduction 'allows the misconception that scientific discovery is an inductive process' (Medawar, 1964, cited in Dubois, 1992: 2).

The process of reconstituting and transforming actual experience for rhetorical purposes is documented as early as the era of Newton (Bazerman, 1988), who deliberately forged verbal means to disarm critics of his Opticks because 'forceful criticism must be attended to with a compelling answer' and 'the text must appear to be the right answer'. (Dubois, 1992: 4)

The rhetorical structure of the text facilitates clarification of the authors' reasoning to the point that replication is unnecessary. Since there is no financial incentive for scientists to replicate one another's experiments, the reader must be able to follow the logic of the thought processes involved (Dubois, 1992). Thus, 'virtual witnessing' is no less a factor than it was in the seventeenth century. This factor is reinforced by prescriptions to the Methods writer to put down exactly what s/he did and in enough detail for the reader to judge whether the findings provide reliable support for the conclusion (e.g. Huth, 1982, cited in Dubois, 1992).

Limitations

The findings for the specific systems (genre structures, lexical cohesion, reference systems and boundary marking systems) are based upon a small number of texts, drawn randomly from the four most frequently cited journals. These journals may not be representative of all social science journals but should be representative of highly valued social science texts.

The question of where one genre ends and another begins is also problematic. We already know that 'scientific writing', even if restricted to research reports, is not a unified whole. Are social science research reports a genre or a subgenre of scientific writing? Are the disciplines we studied (psychology and sociology) a subgenre of social science writing? Our view is that certain basic structures will be similar to all research reports but different disciplines will have their own variations. In the same way, there may be a genre of service encounters that shares elements but will yield great variations in options, depending on whether the encounter is in a travel agency or a post office.

Whether our texts represent a genre or a subgenre seems unimportant. For practical purposes, a description of a genre should be as specific as possible. A description that would include disciplines from astronomy to zoology would be so general that it would be useless.

Implications

Methodological problems in discourse analysis

1. The approach initiated in this study suggests that lexicogrammatical structures should be distinguished from discourse structures and that criteria for identifying discourse units must be rigorous so that future

analyses of the genre of research texts can be carried out within a common working model.

2. Reference systems for tracking participants in a text need to be refined, since existing methods were inadequate for analysing the genre at hand. (This problem is discussed in Chapter 6.) A possible solution is to recognize two functions within reference. The first, a tracking system, composed of articles, personal references and demonstrative references, can follow a particular participant through the text (*John . . . the man . . . he*). The second system, an identifying system, composed of references of relationship, can relate new participants to previously mentioned participants or concurrent information (*A problem . . . a related problem*).

Questions of rhetorical functions in science

1. Distinctions between Introduction, Methods, Results and Discussion seem to be more prescriptive than descriptive. In two texts in the present corpus, much of the Introduction was devoted to Methods. Thompson (1993) reports a high incidence of evaluative statements in Results sections in biochemistry articles, in which biochemists explicitly argue for the validity of their experimental data by employing such moves as: justifying methods; interpreting results; evaluating; citing agreement with the literature and admitting interpretive perplexities and discrepancies. Similar findings were reported by Brett (1994) for Results sections of sociology texts. This trend should be studied further and its implications would be very valuable for those interested in the rhetoric of science, particularly instructors of novice science writers.

2. While this study has focused on prototypical moves and their common features, we have described some of the possible individual acts in realizing these moves. But a more detailed analysis is called for on specific acts such as how authors apologize, accept mistakes or praise their own research. Are these kinds of acts contingent on any other factors? What are the analogies between these acts and parallel acts in face-to-face communication? In particular, the act of giving criticism deserves a separate study in the light of some contradictory findings. On the one hand, the criticisms in this corpus are tempered by 'politeness' and face-saving; on the other hand, harsh criticisms can easily be found in research texts outside this corpus. Is the type of criticism a function of the writer, academic field, e.g. sociology vs. linguistics, academic fashion, or mode, or a combination of several elements? Is it possible that writers of books are allowed more leeway in expressing personal judgements than are authors of journal articles? Among journals, do some allow more criticism than others? This is clearly an area that is worth pursuing further.

3. Analyses of prototypical structures should be extended to other social sciences such as anthropology, economics and political science, to determine the characteristics of each.

4. The next intriguing question is whether these findings extend to texts in

physical sciences. Previous literature has speculated on the extra rhetorical work SSR texts have to do to compensate for being 'soft' sciences. Crookes (1986: 67) found that SSR texts tended to have much longer and more complex introductions than the other sciences, which he claimed reflected a 'lack of shared preconceptions and a greater need for both definition of terms and motivation of hypotheses'. Perhaps our methods can be applied to the study of 'hard' science so that comparisons can be made.

In every sense, a scientific research text is an argument although, theoretically, only reporting results is necessary for establishing one's contribution to science. Moves B–E ('evaluate congruence of findings to other criteria', 'offer interpretation', 'ward off potential counterclaims', 'state implications') have mainly rhetorical functions in convincing the reader of the validity of the claims. The next step would be to understand how these particular moves developed and their place in establishing and reinforcing scientific claims. Furthermore, since not all moves are realized in every text, speculation is in order as to the kinds of factors that motivate particular moves, for instance, whether a majority or a minority view of the field is being posited or whether the authors are novices or more esteemed veteran members of the profession.

5. Although this study has focused on texts, several findings indicate the need to focus on the reader, particularly how s/he processes ambiguity. For instance, we found that, in rare instances, participants undergo a change of status from uncertain to certain upon subsequent mention. In a few cases, a tendency in the Results is transformed to a generalization in the Discussion, or speculation at first mention becomes a fact at second mention. This phenomenon should be studied carefully; if it is shown to be a common practice, it could have very strong implications for those readers who skip the Results section and concentrate on the Discussion section. Some of the additional questions that remain to be studied are:
   a. How does the reader process statements that are simultaneously marked for certainty and uncertainty, e.g. 'It seems clear that . . .'?
   b. In the absence of appropriate markers of conclusion, of hypotheses, and of boundaries, how does the reader recognize rhetorical functions and boundaries? What are the differences in stumbling blocks for the expert and the student reader or writer? Does the expert reader rely on knowledge of the field to recognize boundaries?
   c. What additional difficulties are present for those readers and writers for whom English is a foreign language?

These are important questions, particularly in the light of the increasing number of native and non-native speaker students entering scientific fields. Since scientific writing changes and is adapted to different situations, we need to research the variability. By knowing the details of the range of scientific discourse, researchers and teachers of academic writing can prepare students to integrate successfully into the scientific community.

Bibliography

American Psychological Association (1983), *Publications Manual*, 3rd edition. Washington, DC: APA.

Ard, J. (1983), 'The role of the author in scientific discourse', paper given at the Annual American Applied Linguistics Meeting, Minneapolis, MN, December.

Bakhtin, M. M. (1990), *The Dialogic Imagination*, edited by M. Holquist, translated by C. Emerson and M. Holquist. Austin: University of Texas Press.

Barnard, N. and Kaufman, S. (1997), 'Animal research is wasteful and misleading', *Scientific American*, February, 64–9.

Bazerman, C. (1984), 'The writing of scientific non-fiction', *Pre/text*, 5, 39–65.

Bazerman, C. (1985), 'Physicists reading physics: schema-laden purposes and purpose-laden schema', *Written Communication*, 2, 3–24.

Bazerman, C. (1987a), 'Literate acts and the emergent social structure of science: a critical synthesis', *Social Epistemology*, 1, 295–310.

Bazerman, C. (1987b), 'Codifying the social scientific style: the APA Publication Manual as a behaviorist rhetoric', in D. N. McCloskey (ed.), *The Human Sciences: Language and Argument in Scholarship*. Madison: University of Wisconsin Press.

Bazerman, C. (1988), *Shaping Written Knowledge: The Genre and Activity of the Experimental Article in Science*, Madison: University of Wisconsin Press.

Belanger, M. (1982), 'A preliminary analysis of the structure of the discussion sections in ten neuroscience journal articles' (mimeo).

Bem, D. (1987), 'The journal article', in M. Zanna and J. Darley (eds), *The Compleat Academic: A Practical Guide for the Beginning Social Scientist*. New York: Random House.

Benson, J. and Greaves, W. (eds) (1985), *Systemic Perspectives on Discourse*, Vol. 2. Norwood, NJ: Ablex.

Berkenkotter, C. and Huckin, T. (1995), *Genre in Disciplinary Communication*. Hillsdale, NJ: Erlbaum.

Berry, M. (1981), 'Systemic linguistics and discourse analysis: a multi-layered approach to exchange structure', in M. Coulthard and M. Montgomery (eds), *Studies in Discourse Analysis*. London: Routledge and Kegan Paul.

Bhatia, V. K. (1993), *Analysing Genre*. New York: Longman.

Brett, P. (1994), 'A genre analysis of the results section of sociology articles', *English for Specific Purposes*, 13/1, 47–59.

Brown, G. and Yule, G. (1983), *Discourse Analysis*. Cambridge: Cambridge University Press

Brown, P. and Levinson, S. C. (1987), *Politeness: Some Universals in Language Usage*. Cambridge: Cambridge University Press.

Bruner, E. M. (1986), 'Ethnography as narrative', in V. Turner and E. M. Bruner (eds), *The Anthropology of Experience*. Urbana: University of Illinois.

Campbell, K. and Jamieson, K. (1978), 'Form and genre in rhetorical criticism: an introduction', in K. Campbell and K. Jamieson (eds), *Form and Genre: Shaping Rhetorical Action*. Falls Church, VA: The Speech Communication Association.

Coulthard, M. and Montgomery, M. (eds) (1981), *Studies in Discourse Analysis*. London: Routledge and Kegan Paul.

Couture, B. (1985), 'A systemic network for analyzing writing quality', in J. Benson and W. Greaves (eds), 67–87.

Couture, B. (1986), 'Effective ideation in written text: a functional approach to clarity and exigence', in B. Couture (ed.), *Functional Approaches to Writing: Research Perspectives*. Norwood, NJ: Ablex.

Crookes, G. (1986), 'Towards a validated analysis of scientific text structure', *Applied Linguistics*, 7, 57–69.

de Beaugrande, R. and Dressler, W. (1981), *Introduction to Text Linguistics*. Harlow: Longman.

Dubois, B. L. (1992), 'From narrative toward exposition: materials and methods sections of biomedical journal articles', in R. Merriweather and S.-J. Huang (eds), *Festschrift for R. E. Longacre*. Dallas: Summer Institute for Linguistics and the University of Texas-Arlington.

Dubois, B. L. (1997), *The Biomedical Discussion Section in Context*. Advances in Discourse Processes Series. Greenwich, CT: Ablex.

Dudley-Evans, T. (1986), 'Genre analysis: an investigation of the introduction sections of MSc Dissertions', in M. Coulthard (ed.), *Talking about Text*. Birmingham: University of Birmingham.

Dudley-Evans, T. (1994), 'Genre analysis: an approach to text analysis for ESP', in M. Coulthard (ed.), *Advances in Written Text Analysis*. London: Routledge.

Fawcett, R. (1980), *Cognitive Linguistics and Social Interaction: Towards an Integrated Model of a Systemic Functional Grammar and the Other Components of an Interacting Mind*. Heidelberg: Julius Groos.

Fine, J. (1978), 'Conversation, cohesive and thematic patterning in children's dialogues', *Discourse Processes*, 1, 247–66.

Fine, J. (1994), *How Language Works: Cohesion in Normal and Nonstandard Communication*. Norwood, NJ: Ablex.

Fortanet, I., Posteguillo, S., Palmer, J. C. and Coll, J. F. (eds) (1998), *Genre Studies in English for Academic Purposes*. Castello: Publicacions de la Universitat Jaume I.

Freedman, A. (1993), 'Show and tell? The role of explicit teaching in the learning of new genres', *Research in the Teaching of English*, Vol. 27, 222–51.

Freedman, A. and Medway, P. (eds) (1994), *Genre and the New Rhetoric*. London: Taylor and Francis Ltd.

Garfield, E. (ed.) (1981), *Science Citation Index*. Philadelphia: ISI.

Garfield, E. (ed.) (1982), *Science Citation Index*. Philadelphia: ISI.

Gilbert, G. N. and Mulkay, M. (1984), *Opening Pandora's Box: Sociological Analysis of Scientists' Discourse*. Cambridge: Cambridge University Press.

Gnutzmann, C. and Oldenburg, H. (1991), 'Contrastive text linguistics in LSP-research: theoretical considerations and some preliminary findings', in H. Schroder (ed.), *Subject Oriented Texts: Languages for Special Purposes and Text Theory*. Berlin: de Gruyter.

Golebiowski, Z. (1998), 'Rhetorical approaches to scientific writing : an English–Polish contrastive study', *Text*, 18, 67–102.

Gregory, M. (1967), 'Aspects of varieties differentiation', *Journal of Linguistics*, 3, 177–98.

Gregory, M. (1988), 'Generic situation and register: a functional view of communication', in J. D. Benson, M. J. Cummings and W. S. Greaves (eds), *Linguistics in a Systemic Perspective*. Amsterdam/Philadelphia: John Benjamins, 301–29.

Gregory, M. and Carroll, S. (1978), *Language and Situation: Language Varieties and Their Social Contexts*. London: Routledge and Kegan Paul.

Grimes, J. (1975), *The Thread of Discourse*. The Hague: Mouton.

Grimes, J. (ed.) (1978), *Papers on Discourse*. Dallas: Summer Institute of Linguistics.

Grosz, B. J. (1982), 'Discourse analysis', in R. Kittredge and J. Lehrberger (eds), *Sublanguage: Studies of Language in Restricted Semantic Domains*. Berlin: de Gruyter (first published 1975).

Halliday, M. A. K. (1965) 'Speech and situation', *Bulletin of the National Association for the Teaching of English: Some Aspects of Oracy*, 2(2), 14–17.

Halliday, M. A. K. (1973), *Explorations in the Functions of Language*, New York: Elsevier North Holland.

Halliday, M. A. K. (1978), *Language as Social Semiotic: The Social Interpretation of Language and Meaning*. London: Edward Arnold.

Halliday, M. A. K. (1985), *An Introduction to Functional Grammar*. London: Edward Arnold.

Halliday, M. A. K. (1988), 'On the language of physical science', in M. Ghadessy (ed.), *Registers of Written English Situational Factors and Linguistic Features*. London: Pinter.

Halliday, M. A. K. (1997), 'Linguistics as metaphor', in A.-M. Simon-Vandenbergen, K. Davidse and D. Noel, *Reconnecting Language: Morphology and Syntax in Functional Perspectives*. Amsterdam: John Benjamins.

Halliday, M. A. K. and Hasan, R. (1976), *Cohesion in English*. London: Longman.

Halliday, M. A. K. and Hasan, R. (1985), *Language, Context and Text: Aspects of Language in a Social-Semiotic Perspective*. Victoria: Deakin University Press.

Hasan, R. (1977), 'Text in the systemic-functional model', in W. Dressler (ed.), *Current Trends in Text Linguistics*. Berlin: Walter de Gruyter.

Hasan, R. (1984), 'The nursery tale as a genre', *Nottingham Linguistic Circular*, 13, 71–102.

Hasan, R. (ed.) (1985), *Discourse on Discourse*. Wollongong, NSW: Applied Linguistics Association of Australia.

Hoey, M. (1979), *Signalling in Discourse*. Birmingham: English Language Research Unit, University of Birmingham.

Hoey, M. (1983), *On the Surface of Discourse*. London: George Allen and Unwin.

Holmes, R. (1997), 'Genre analysis and the social sciences: an investigation of the structure of research article discussion sections in three disciplines', *English for Specific Purposes*, 16, 321–37.

Holtgraves, J. (1986), 'Language structure in social interaction', *Journal of Personality and Social Psychology*, 51, 305–14.

Hopkins, A. and Dudley-Evans, T. (1988), 'A genre-based investigation of the discussion sections in articles and dissertations', *English for Specific Purposes*, 7, 113–21.

Huckin, T. N. (1987), 'Surprise value in scientific discourse', Paper presented at the CCC Convention, Atlanta, GA, March.

Huth, E. J. (1982), *How to Write and Publish Papers in the Medical Sciences*. Philadelphia: ISI Press.

Hyland, K. (1996), 'Writing without conviction? Hedging in science research articles', *Applied Linguistics*, 17, 433–54.

Hyland, K. (1998), 'Boosting, hedging and the negotiation of academic knowledge', *Text*, 18, 348–82.

Journet, D. (1990), 'Writing, rhetoric and the social construction of scientific knowledge', *IEEE Transactions on Professional Communication*, 33/4, 162–7.

Kerlinger, F. N. (1973), *Foundations of Behavioral Research*. New York: Holt, Rinehart and Winston.

Kinneavy, J. (1971), *A Theory of Discourse*. New York: W. W. Norton.

Knorr-Certina, K. D. (1981), *The Manufacture of Knowledge*. Oxford: Pergamon.

Kong, K. (1998), 'Are simple business request letters really simple? A comparison of Chinese and English business request letters', *Text*, 18, 104–41.

Labov, W. and Waletzky, J. (1967), 'Narrative analysis: oral versions of personal experience', in J. Helm (ed.), *Essays on the Verbal and Visual Arts*. Philadelphia: American Ethnological Society.

Larsen-Freeman, D. and Long, M. H. (1990), *An Introduction to Second Language Acquisition Research*. London: Longman.

Leckie-Tarry, H. (1995), *Language and Context: A Functional Theory of Register* (D. Birch, ed.). London: Pinter.

Lewin, B. A. (1994), *A Genre-Based Approach to Scientific Reports: The Analysis of Social Science Research Texts*. Unpublished doctoral dissertation, Bar-Ilan University, Ramat-Gan, Israel.

Lewin, B. A. and Fine, J. (1996), 'The writing of research texts: genre analysis and its application', in G. Rijlaarsdam, H. Van den Bergh and M. Couzijn (eds), *Theories, Models and Methodology in Writing Research*. Amsterdam: Amsterdam University Press.

Link, C. (1978), 'Units in Wobe discourse', in J. Grimes (ed.).

Lloyd, S. M. (ed.) (1986), *Roget's Thesaurus of English Words and Phrases*. Harmondsworth: Penguin Books.

Lyotard, J.-F. (1979), *The Postmodern Condition: A Report on Knowledge* (G. Bennington and B. Massumi, trans.). Minneapolis: University of Minnesota Press.

Malinowski, B. (1935), *Coral Gardens and their Magic*, Vol. 2. London: Allen and Unwin. Reprinted (1967) as *The Language of Magic and Gardening* (Indiana University Studies in the History and Theory of Linguistics). Bloomington: Indiana University Press.

Mann, W. C. and Thompson, S. A. (1988), 'Rhetorical structure theory: toward a functional theory of text organisation', *Text*, 8, 242–81.

Markkanen, R. and Schröder, H. (1987), 'Hedging and its linguistic realizations in German, English and Finnish philosophical texts: a case study', *Subject Oriented Texts and Theory of Translation*, VAKKI seminar, Voyri, Finland, 31.1–1.2.87.

Martin, J. R. (1983), 'Conjunction: the logic of English text', in J. S. Petofi and E. Sozer (eds), *Micro and Macro Connexity of Texts*. Hamburg: Helmut Buske Verlag.

Martin, J. R. (1985), 'Process and text: two aspects of human semiosis', in J. D. Benson and W. S. Greaves (eds), 248–74.

Martin, J. R. (1992), *English Text: System and Structure*. Amsterdam: John Benjamins.

Martin, J. R. and Peters, P. (1985), 'On the analysis of exposition', in R. Hasan (ed.), 61–92.

McKinlay, J. (1982), *An Analysis of Discussion Sections in Medical Journal Articles*. Unpublished MA thesis, University of Birmingham.

Medawar, P. (1964), 'Is the scientific paper fraudulent?', *Saturday Review*, Aug. 1, 42–3.

Meyer, B. J. F. and Freedle, R. O. (1984), 'Effects of discourse type on recall', *American Educational Research Journal*, 21, 121–43.

Meyer, B. J. F. and Rice, E. (1984), 'The structure of text', in P. D. Pearson (ed.), *Handbook of Reading Research*. New York: Longman.

Miller, C. (1994), 'Genre as social action', in A. Freedman and P. Medway (eds).

Myers, G. (1985), 'The social construction of two biologists' proposals', *Written Communication*, 2/3, 1–35.

Myers, G. (1989), 'The pragmatics of politeness in scientific articles', *Applied Linguistics*, 10, 1–35.

Myers, G. (1990), *Writing Biology: Texts in the Social Construction of Scientific Knowledge*. Madison: University of Wisconsin.

Myers, G. (1992), ' "In this paper we report . . .": speech acts and scientific facts', *Journal of Pragmatics*, 17, 295–313.

Nwogu, K. N. (1997), 'The medical research paper: structure and functions', *English for Specific Purposes*, 16, 119–38.

Paltridge, B. (1997), *Genre, Frames and Writing in Research Settings*. Philadelphia: John Benjamins.

Peng, J. (1987), 'Organizational features in chemical engineering research articles', *ELR Journal* (University of Birmingham), 1, 79–116.

Popper, K. R. (1963), *Conjectures and Refutations*. London: Routledge and Kegan Paul.

Quirk, R., Greenbaum, S., Leech, G. and Svartvik, J. (1991), *A Grammar of Contemporary English*. Harlow: Longman.

Richardson, L. (1990), *Writing Strategies: Reaching Diverse Audiences*, Qualitative Research Method Series 21. Newbury Park, CA: Sage.

Samraj, B. T. R. (1989), 'Exploring current issues in genre theory', *Word*, 40/1–2, 189–200.

Schottelndreyer, B. (1978), 'Narrative discourse in Sherpa', in J. Grimes (ed.).

Searle, J. (1969), *Speech Acts: An Essay in the Philosophy of Language*. Cambridge: Cambridge University Press.

Shadish, W. and Fuller, S. (1994), *The Social Psychology of Science*. New York: Guilford Press.

Shapin, S. (1984), 'Pump and circumstance: Robert Boyle's literary technology', *Social Studies of Science*, 14, 481–520.

Sinclair, J. M. and Coulthard, M. (1975), *Towards an Analysis of Discourse*. Oxford: Oxford University Press.

Sperber, D. and Wilson, D. (1986), *Relevance*. Oxford: Blackwell.

Swales, J. (1981), *Aspects of Article Introductions*. Birmingham: University of Aston, Language Studies Unit.

Swales, J. (1987), 'Utilizing the Literature in Teaching the Research Paper', *TESOL Quarterly*, 21, 41–68.

Swales, J. (1990), *Genre Analysis*. Cambridge: Cambridge University Press.

Swales, J. and Najjar, H. (1987), 'The writing of research article introductions', *Written Communication*, 4, 175–91.

Thompson, D. (1993), 'Arguing for experimental "facts" in science: a study of research article results sections in biochemistry', *Written Communication*, 10, 106–28.

Valle, E. (1997), 'A scientific community and its texts: a historical discourse study', in B.-L. Gunnarsson, P. Linell and B. Nordberg (eds), *The Construction of Professional Discourse*. London: Longman.

Ventola, E. (1984), 'Orientation to social semiotics in foreign language teaching', *Applied Linguistics*, 5, 275–86.

Ventola, E. (1987), *The Structure of Social Interaction: A Systematic Approach to the Semiotics of Service Encounters*. London: Pinter.

Ventola, E. (1988), 'Text analysis in operation: a multilevel approach', in R. Fawcett and D. Young (eds), *New Developments in Systemic Linguistics*. London: Pinter.

Ventola, E. (1989), 'Problems of modelling and applied issues within the framework of genre', *Word*, 40, 129–61.

Ventola, E. and Mauranen, A. (1991), 'Non-native writing and native revising of scientific articles', in E. Ventola (ed.), *Functional and Systemic Linguistics*. Berlin: Mouton de Gruyter.

Weimar, W. B. (1977), 'Science as a rhetorical transaction: toward a nonjustificational conception of rhetoric', *Philosophy and Rhetoric*, 10, 1–30.

Williams, J. and Colomb, G. (1993), 'The case for explicit teaching: why what you don't know won't help you', *Research in the Teaching of English*, 27, 252–63.

Yang, A. (1989), 'Cohesive chains and writing quality', *Word*, 40 (1–2), 235–54.

Young L. (1990), *Language as Behaviour, Language as Code: A Study of Academic English*. Amsterdam: John Benjamins.

Texts used for analysis

1. Shepelak, N. and Alwin, D. F. (1986), 'Beliefs about inequality and perceptions of distributive justice', *American Sociological Review*, 51, 30–46.

2. Miethe, T. D., Stafford, M. C. and Long, J. S. (1987), 'Social differentiation in criminal victimization: a test of routine activities/lifestyle theories, *American Sociological Review*, 52, 184–94.

3. Hughes, J. R. and Hatsukami, D. (1986), 'Signs and symptoms of tobacco withdrawal', *Archives of General Psychiatry*, 43, 289–94.

4. Solomon, C., Holzman, P. S., Levin, S. and Gale, H. J. (1987), 'The association between eye-tracking dysfunctions and thought disorder in psychosis', *Archives of General Psychiatry*, 44, 31–5.

5. Colombo, J. and Horowitz, F. (1986), 'Infants' attentional responses to frequency modulated sweeps', *Child Development*, 57, 287–91.

6. Ladd, G. W. and Price, J. M. (1987), 'Predicting children's social and school adjustment following the transition from preschool to kindergarten', *Child Development*, 58, 1168–89.

7. Mullen, B., Futrell, D., Stairs, D., Tice, D., Dawson, K., Riordan, C., Kennedy, J., Baumeister, R., Radloff, C., Goethals, G. and Rosenfeld, P. (1986), 'Newscasters' facial expressions and voting behavior of viewers: can a smile elect a president?', *Journal of Personality and Social Psychology*, 51, 291–5.

8. Lehmann, D., Wortmann, C. and Williams, A. (1987), 'Long-term effects of losing a spouse or child in a motor vehicle crash', *Journal of Personality and Social Psychology*, 52, 218–31.

9. Lin, N. and Ensel, W. M. (1989), 'Life stress and health: stressors and resources', *American Sociological Review*, 54, 382–99.

10. Griffin, M. L., Weiss, R. D., Mirin, S. M. and Lange, U. (1989), 'A comparison of male and female cocaine abusers', *Archives of General Psychiatry*, 46, 122–6.

11. Fagot, B. I. and Leinbach, M. D. (1989), 'The young child's gender schema: environmental input, internal organization', *Child Development*, 60, 663–72.

12. Duclos, S. E., Laird, J. D., Schneider, E., Sexter, M., Stern, L. and Van Lighten, O. (1989), 'Emotion-specific effects of facial expressions and postures on emotional experience', *Journal of Personality and Social Psychology*, 57, 100–08.

13. Gottman, J. and Leveson, R. W. (1992), 'Marital processes predictive of later dissolution: behavior, physiology and health', *Journal of Personality and Social Psychology*, 63, 221–33.

14. Hout, M. (1984), 'Occupational mobility of black men: 1962–1973', *American Sociological Review*, 49, 308–22.

15. Ditto, P. and Lopez, D. (1992), 'Motivated skepticism: use of differential decision criteria for preferred and non-preferred conclusions', *Journal of Personality and Social Psychology*, 63, 568–84.

Index